Parts of an insect

All insects have the following things in common:
1 An outside skeleton (or exo-skeleton)
2 Three pairs of jointed legs
3 A body divided into three sections:
   head, thorax and abdomen
4 External mouthparts on their head

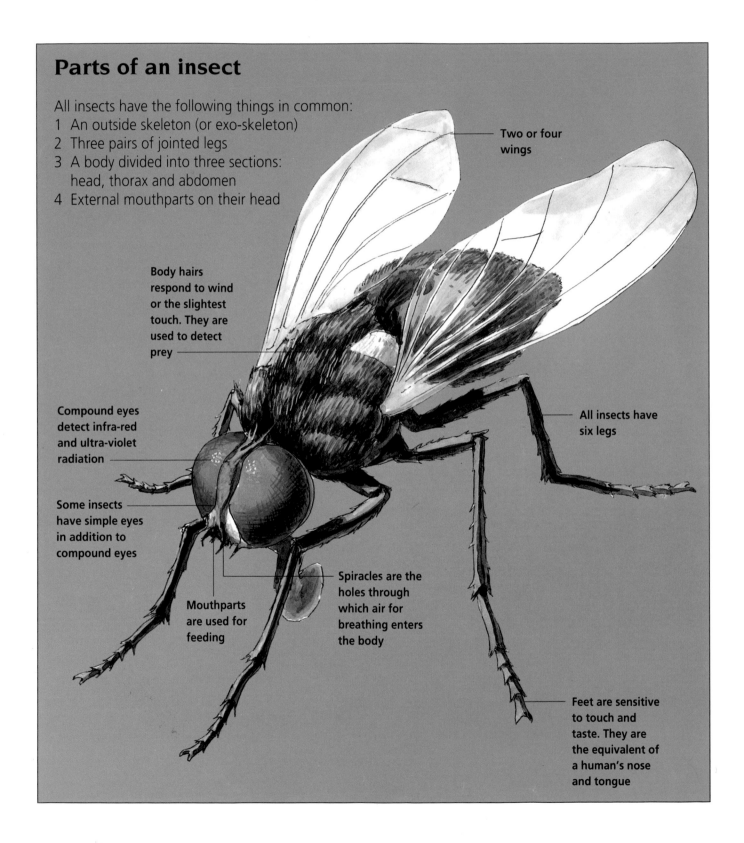

Two or four wings

Body hairs respond to wind or the slightest touch. They are used to detect prey

Compound eyes detect infra-red and ultra-violet radiation

All insects have six legs

Some insects have simple eyes in addition to compound eyes

Mouthparts are used for feeding

Spiracles are the holes through which air for breathing enters the body

Feet are sensitive to touch and taste. They are the equivalent of a human's nose and tongue

INSECTS

George C. McGavin

EDITED BY
Leslie Jackman

DRAGON'S WORLD

CHILDREN'S BOOKS

Conservation

There are about 200,000 individual insects for every one human on the Earth. Most insects live in the tropics, and over half of them live in tropical rain forests. The other place that many different insects live is in wetlands, which includes areas like flood plains, marshes and swamps.

Unfortunately these two habitats are the ones that are most at risk in the world today. People are felling the tropical rain forests for the hardwoods, like mahogany, to make furniture, or clearing them for farms. People are draining wetlands, because they are good places to farm once the water has gone. Either way, unique insect species are being lost every day – some scientists estimate the planet is losing over a thousand species a year.

On page 78, you will find the names of some organizations who campaign for the protection of particular animals and habitats in Britain and around the world. By joining them and supporting their efforts, **you** can help to preserve our wildlife.

Insect Hunter's Code

1 **Always go collecting with a friend,** and always tell an adult where you have gone.
2 **Treat all insects with care** – most are delicate creatures and can be easily killed by rough handling.
3 **Leave insects' nests** undisturbed as much as possible.
4 **Ask permission** before exploring or crossing private property. Keep to footpaths as much as possible.
5 **Keep off crops and leave fence gates** as you find them.
6 **Ask your parents only to light fires** in a fireplace in a special picnic area.

Dragon's World Ltd
Limpsfield
Surrey RH8 0DY
Great Britain

First published by Dragon's World 1994

© Dragon's World 1994
© Text Dragon's World 1994
© Species illustrations Richard Lewington 1992 & 1994
© Other illustrations Dragon's World 1994

Simplified text and captions by Leslie Jackman, based on *Insects of the Northern Hemisphere* by George C. McGavin.

Species illustrations by Richard Lewington. Habitat paintings by Philip Weare, of Lindon Artists. Headbands by Antonia Phillips. Identification and activities illustrations by Mr Gay Galsworthy.

Editor   Diana Briscoe
Designer   James Lawrence
Design Assistant Victoria Furbisher
Art Director   John Strange
Editorial Director Pippa Rubinstein

British Library
Cataloguing in Publication Data
The catalogue record for this book is available from the British Library.

ISBN 1 85028 237 4

Typeset in Frutiger Light and Novarese Bold by Dragon's World Ltd.
Printed in Spain.

Contents

What is an Insect?

There are over 1.5 million species of animals to be found on Earth, and nearly 932,000 of them are insects. Because there are so many different insects, this book only deals with families of insects, not with their separate species.

Insects are invertebrates, which means that they do not have an internal backbone as fish or snakes or dogs do. The first insects developed between 300 and 400 million years ago – long before even the dinosaurs!

The success of many insects is partly because they can fly. With wings insects can travel long distances to find new habitats and they can escape from their enemies. Some can beat their wings as fast as 1000 beats per second.

There are so many different families of insects, that you will have to look at the specimens you find very carefully to decide which family they belong to. By doing this you will soon discover how wonderfully insects are made.

From egg to insect

Insects are divided into groups, called 'orders' (see pages 5, 6 and 7). The most advanced insect orders, like Coleoptera or Lepidoptera, have a very complicated life cycle during which they change their shape three times. Each time they look completely different from their previous shape. How this works is shown in the picture. The fly life cycle can be as short as 14 days; the adults will live several weeks.

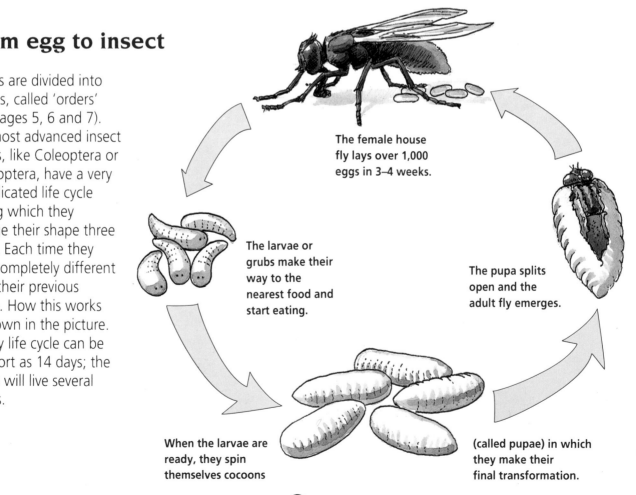

The female house fly lays over 1,000 eggs in 3–4 weeks.

The larvae or grubs make their way to the nearest food and start eating.

When the larvae are ready, they spin themselves cocoons

(called pupae) in which they make their final transformation.

The pupa splits open and the adult fly emerges.

Orders for insects

There are nearly 932,000 species of insects, subdivided into smaller groups called Orders. There are over twenty-five Orders, but as over 1,000 new species of insects are described every year, this is constantly changing. These are the largest Orders:

COLEOPTERA
Beetles
(about 370,000)

LEPIDOPTERA
Butterflies & Moths
(about 165,000)

HYMENOPTERA
Sawflies, Bees,
Wasps & Ants
(about 120,000)

HEMIPTERA
Bugs, Hoppers
& Aphids
(about 90,000)

ORTHOPTERA
Grasshopper
& Crickets
(about 19,000)

DIPTERA – Flies
(about 119,500)

Habitat Picture Bands

This book is divided into different habitats (type of countryside). Each habitat has a different picture band at the top of the page. These are shown below.

Found Almost Everywhere

Meadows & Fields

Woodlands

Rivers, Lakes & Bogs

Pests & Parasites

How to use this book

This book will introduce you to some of the more common families of insects. Each family has an entry and a picture of a typical insect from the family. When trying to identify the insect you have found, expect that it will look something like the picture, but not be exactly the same. To identify an insect, follow these steps.

1 **Look at the list of the most common orders and their pictures** shown here. Which does it resemble most? The identification chart on pages 6–7 will help you to decide.

2 **Decide what habitat you are in**. If you aren't sure, read the descriptions at the start of each section to see which one fits best. Each habitat has a different picture band heading and these are shown here.

3 **Look through the pages of insects with this picture band.** The picture and information given for each insect family will help you to identify it. The large winged insect (below) is a Hawkmoth (see page 21).

4 **If you can't find the insect there,** look through the other sections. Some species of an insect family may live in a different habitat. Pests and parasites move with their hosts. You will find the small insect (below) is a Diving Beetle (see page 61).

5 **If you still can't find the insect** you may have to look in a larger field guide (see page 78 for some suggestions.) You might have spotted something very rare or even unknown!

What Is It?

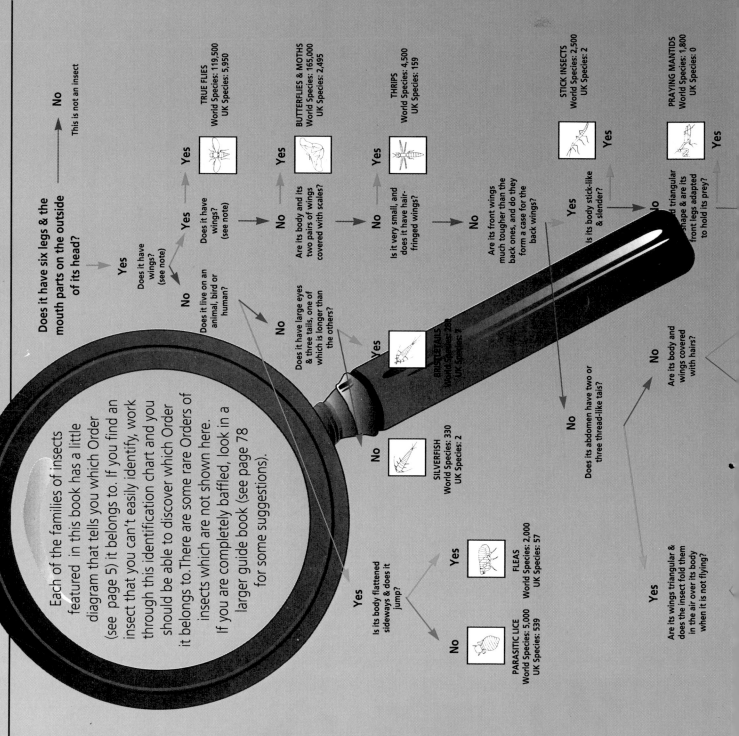

Each of the families of insects featured in this book has a little diagram that tells you which Order (see page 5) it belongs to. If you find an insect that you can't easily identify, work through this identification chart and you should be able to discover which Order it belongs to. There are some rare Orders of insects which are not shown here. If you are completely baffled, look in a larger guide book (see page 78 for some suggestions).

Does it have six legs & the mouth parts on the outside of its head?

No → This is not an insect

Yes → **Does it have wings?** (see note)

Yes → **Does it have wings?** (see note)

Yes → **TRUE FLIES**
World Species: 119,500
UK Species: 5,950

No → **Are its body and its two pairs of wings covered with scales?**

Yes → **BUTTERFLIES & MOTHS**
World Species: 165,000
UK Species: 2,495

No → **Is it very small, and does it have hair-fringed wings?**

Yes → **THRIPS**
World Species: 4,500
UK Species: 159

No → **Are its front wings much tougher than the back ones, and do they form a case for the back wings?**

Yes → **Is its body stick-like & slender?**

Yes → **STICK INSECTS**
World Species: 2,500
UK Species: 2

No → ...triangular shape & are its front legs adapted to hold its prey?

Yes → **PRAYING MANTIDS**
World Species: 1,800
UK Species: 0

No → **Does it live on an animal, bird or human?**

No → **Does it have large eyes & three tails, one of which is longer than the others?**

Yes → **BRISTLETAILS**
World Species: 280
UK Species: 7

No → **SILVERFISH**
World Species: 330
UK Species: 2

Yes → **Is its body flattened sideways & does it jump?**

Yes → **FLEAS**
World Species: 2,000
UK Species: 57

No → **PARASITIC LICE**
World Species: 5,000
UK Species: 539

No → **Does its abdomen have two or three thread-like tails?**

No → **Are its body and wings covered with hairs?**

Yes → **Are its wings triangular & does the insect fold them in the air over its body when it is not flying?**

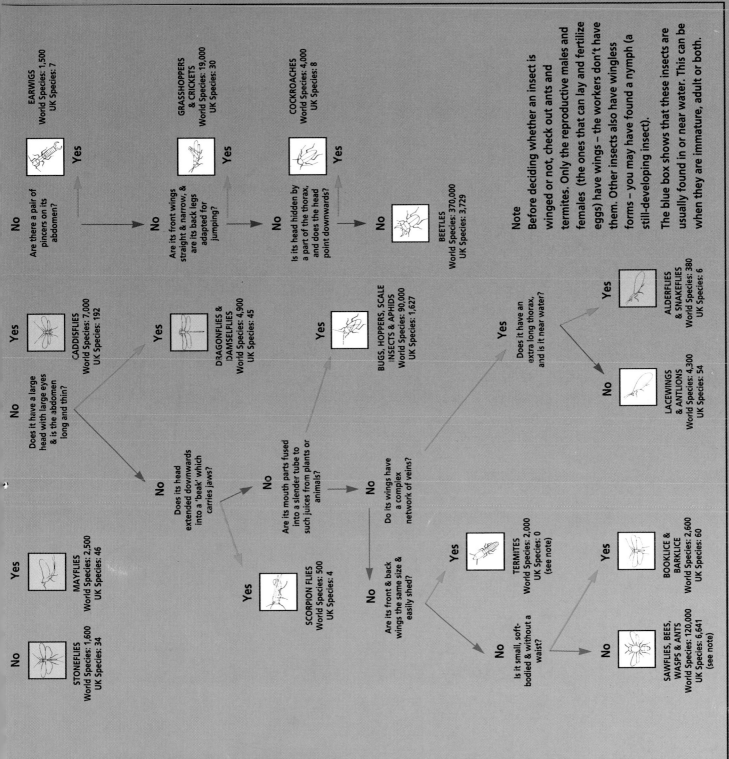

No — **STONEFLIES** World Species: 1,600 UK Species: 34

Yes — **MAYFLIES** World Species: 2,500 UK Species: 46

Does it have a large head with large eyes & is the abdomen long and thin?

Yes — **CADDISFLIES** World Species: 7,000 UK Species: 192

No — Does its head extended downwards into a 'beak' which carries jaws?

Yes — **DRAGONFLIES & DAMSELFLIES** World Species: 4,900 UK Species: 45

Yes — **SCORPION FLIES** World Species: 500 UK Species: 4

No — Are its mouth parts fused into a slender tube to such juices from plants or animals?

Yes — **BUGS, HOPPERS, SCALE INSECTS & APHIDS** World Species: 90,000 UK Species: 1,627

No — Do its wings have a complex network of veins?

Yes — Does it have an extra long thorax, and is it near water?

Yes — **ALDERFLIES & SNAKEFLIES** World Species: 380 UK Species: 6

No — **LACEWINGS & ANTLIONS** World Species: 4,300 UK Species: 54

No — Are its front & back wings the same size & easily shed?

Yes — **TERMITES** World Species: 2,000 UK Species: 0 (see note)

No — Is it small, soft-bodied & without a waist?

Yes — **BOOKLICE & BARKLICE** World Species: 2,600 UK Species: 60

No — **SAWFLIES, BEES, WASPS & ANTS** World Species: 120,000 UK Species: 6,641 (see note)

No — Are there a pair of pincers on its abdomen?

Yes — **EARWIGS** World Species: 1,500 UK Species: 7

No — Are its front wings straight & narrow, & are its back legs adapted for jumping?

Yes — **GRASSHOPPERS & CRICKETS** World Species: 19,000 UK Species: 30

No — Is its head hidden by a part of the thorax, and does the head point downwards?

Yes — **COCKROACHES** World Species: 4,000 UK Species: 8

No — **BEETLES** World Species: 370,000 UK Species: 3,729

Note

Before deciding whether an insect is winged or not, check out ants and termites. Only the reproductive males and females (the ones that can lay and fertilize eggs) have wings – the workers don't have them. Other insects also have wingless forms – you may have found a nymph (a still-developing insect).

The blue box shows that these insects are usually found in or near water. This can be when they are immature, adult or both.

Found Almost Everywhere

The families that you will find in the following pages are either very common indeed or truly widespread. You will easily find many of them in parks and gardens, but most you may see everywhere from a city street to a seaside beach – and anywhere in between!

Gardens and parks are a very important habitat (type of landscape) for wildlife, especially now that gardeners are planting such a wide variety of plants. Different plants lead to lots of different insects, many of whom only eat from one type of plant. Lots of insects encourage more insectivores, like birds and hedgehogs, to live in the area.

Did you know that the total area of urban gardens in England and Wales is well over a million acres? That is more than three times the area of all Britain's national nature reserves.

A well-stocked, average-sized, urban garden (measuring about 200 square metres) may hold 200–300 different beetle species, up to 200 species of flies, of which more than 50–60 may be hover flies, and hundreds of Hymenoptera species, including sixty or more species of solitary bees and wasps. In addition there may be 80–90 bug species, and more than 300 butterflies and moths (mostly moths). And remember, many of those insects may be simply passing through as tourists. This picture shows nine insects from this section; see how many you can identify.

Aphid, Bumble Bee, Earwig, Geometrid Moth, Hover Fly, Lady bird, Plant Bug, Weevil, White Butterfly.

Spittle Bugs

In summer you have probably seen a small, white, frothy mass on the plant stems. It is often called 'cuckoo spit'. If you take a grass stem and gently stroke away the bubbles, you will discover the nymph of a spittle bug. The foam, which acts as a sort of bubble-nest protection, is a gland secretion mixed with water. Some birds have learned to pull the nymphs out and eat them. Adult spittle bugs, like froghoppers (see page 41), are active jumpers.

Order: Hemiptera
Family: Aphrophoridae
UK species: 9
World species: 850
Body length: 6–12 mm

Philaenus spumarius (Meadow Spittle Bug)

Jumping Plantlice

Each species belonging to this family lives on one, or a few closely related plants. Some lay stalked eggs on plant surfaces, while others lay eggs inside plants. All this family are important pests because they are sap-suckers. This means that they can transmit virus diseases to plants such as tomatoes, potatoes, apples and pears. *Psylla pyricola* (Pear Sucker, shown here) is a pest on pear crops. Some members of this family also cause galls to form on leaves. Their name refers to their habit of jumping and flying at the smallest disturbance.

Order: Hemiptera
Family: Psyllidae
UK species: 78
World species: 1,500
Body length: 1.5–5 mm

Plantlice, Greenfly or Aphids

You can nearly always see these tiny insects on plants – they are found almost anywhere. They are all suckers of plant sap. Most species give birth to live nymphs. As time passes winged adult aphids appear. They then fly to other plants. Because the nymphs suck in so much sweet plant sap, they produce lots of sugary waste. This 'honeydew' is often collected by ants.

Order: Hemiptera
Family: Aphididae
UK species: 380
World species: 2,250
Body length: 1–8 mm

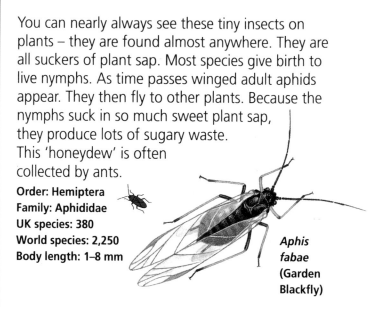

Aphis fabae (Garden Blackfly)

Flower or Minute Pirate Bugs

This is a family that lives in a variety of habitats such as in flowers, under bark, in vegetation, leaf litter and fungi. Others live in mammals' burrows, bird nests, bat caves and grain stores. Many prey on small insects, while others are herbivorous (they eat plants). A few species are viviparous, which means they produce living young. Some species are useful to humans because they eat red spider mites, aphids and scale insects (see page 75).

Order: Hemiptera
Family: Anthocoridae
UK species: 27
World species: 500
Body length: 2–5 mm

Anthocoris confusus

Plant Bugs

A family found in every habitat from ground level to tree tops and on every type of vegetation. This family is the largest of the true bugs. The habits of various species vary enormously. You may come across some by simply looking carefully on plants, or perhaps find some in your beating tray (see pages 62–63). A few species give off scents, which are like the alarm scents given off by ants – a good protective device. Some species can feed on prey caught in spider webs.

Lygus rugulipennis
(European Tarnished Plant Bug)

Order: Hemiptera – Family: Miridae
UK species: 210 – World species: 7,000 – Body length: 1.5–15 mm

Shield or Stink Bugs

Zicrona caerulea
(Blue Bug)

The common names for these insects come from their shield-like shape and their ability to produce very strong-smelling fluids. These fluids repel enemies, can stain skin and even produce bad headaches in sensitive people. Shield bugs live on herbaceous plants, shrubs and trees in a wide range of habitats. Most are plant eaters, but some are carnivorous. In many species the female will guard her eggs and shepherd the young nymphs together, covering them with her body when danger threatens.

Order: Hemiptera – Family: Pentatomidae
UK species: 18 – World species: 5,250 – Body length: 5–35 mm

Assassin & Thread-legged Bugs

Vegetation of all kinds provides habitat for this family. They are well named because they hunt and kill all kinds of insects by sucking out their juices. A few species suck the blood of birds and mammals. Some species lie in wait to ambush prey while others actively hunt for their food. Many species mimic the appearance and colour pattern of their prey. A few assassin bug species collect sticky plant resins on their front legs to attract and snare prey.

Order: Hemiptera
Family: Reduviidae
UK species: 6
World species: 5,500
Body length: 7–40 mm

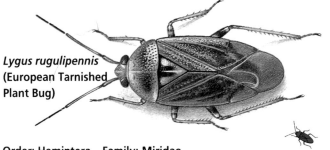

Reduvius personatus
(the Masked Hunter) is sometimes found in houses. It can inflict a painful bite.

Found Almost Everywhere

Ground Beetles

These beetles have well-developed legs and powerful jaws. They live in a wide range of habitats under stones, wood and debris. If you lift such objects, you may see one running away very fast. They catch and eat a large variety of invertebrates and carrion, although a few species feed on plants. Their larvae are also active hunters and live in soil and leaf litter. They have powerful jaws and use enzymes to dissolve their prey's insides. The adults of some species climb into trees and shrubs to catch and eat caterpillars.

Order: Coleoptera
Family: Carabidae
UK species: 330
World species: 25,000
Body length: 2–85 mm

Calosoma sycophanta

Carrion or Burying Beetles

These beetles have a very sensitive sense of smell and are attracted to the dead bodies of animals. The well-named *Nicrophorus vespilloides* (Sexton Beetle, shown here) is a good example of the family. The adult beetles are very strong and two can move an animal as big as a rat to a good location for burying. Their purpose in doing this is to lay eggs on or near the carcass so that the larvae have a plentiful food supply. They are very important in nutrient recycling and carcass disposal – some of the insect refuse collectors of the world.

Order: Coleoptera – Family: Silphidae
UK species: 21 – World species: 250
Body length: 5–40 mm

Rove Beetles

This family has very many species. Most are quite small and run fast. Small species fly by day while larger ones fly at night. This is a family of predators, scavengers or herbivores. By searching under stones you may find a *Staphylinus olens* (Devil's Coach-horse, shown here). 300 species of rove beetles are associated with ants. They mimic their hosts and offer them a sweet fluid to avoid attack, but they prey on hurt or dead ants.

Order: Coleoptera
Family: Staphylinidae
UK species: 825
World species: 27,000
Body length: 1–40 mm

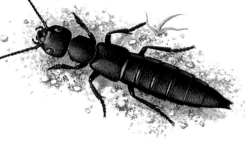

Chequered Beetles

Most of this family have soft, slightly flattened bodies which are very hairy. Their colouring can be bright blue, green, red, brown or pink. Chequered beetles are to be found on the leaves of woody plants and in woody areas. The larvae prey on the larvae of bark beetles and other bark-boring beetles. Some others prey on larvae of bees and wasps, and on grasshopper egg-pods. Some species are able to find their prey by the pheromones (scents) they produce. The *Necrobia rufipes* (Redlegged Ham Beetle, shown here) can damage stored meat and meat products.

Order: Coleoptera
Family: Cleridae
UK species: 10
World species: 3,500
Body length: 2–30 mm

Pollen or Sap Beetles

Look at daisies and their flowers for these beetles. The adults feed on sap oozing from tree wounds, on flower nectar, decaying fruits, carrion and other rotting matter.

Meligethes aeneus (Pollen Beetle)

Some species are associated with ants and bees. Anybody who wears yellow clothes in the summer may find they attract members of this family. They can ruin picnics and also seem to be attracted to bright, fresh paintwork. A few species prey on scale insects, and some feed inside plant seed-pods.

Order: Coleoptera – Family: Nitidulidae
UK species: 95 – World species: 2,800
Body length: 1–14 mm

Leaf Beetles

Members of this family are to be found on every plant species. The adults chew flowers and foliage. Their larvae feed in the same way, but also mine and bore through leaves, stems and roots. Many of these smooth, rounded and often shiny or colourful beetles are serious pests. This is the notorious *Leptinotarsa decemlineata* (Colorado Potato Beetle). Some species can be helpful by controlling weedy plants.

Order: Coleoptera
Family: Chrysomelidae
UK species: 254
World species: 30,000
Body length: 1–35 mm

Darkling Beetles

Many species belonging to this interesting family are adapted to life in very dry conditions, such as deserts and grain stores. Some species produce jets of blistering chemical spray to deter their enemies, but some predatory mammals know this danger. They stick the beetle's spraying tail-end in the ground and eat them head first. Many species have very reduced hind wings, so they do not fly. Mostly they prefer to live in dark places – hence their name. Some are called flour beetles and are pests of cereals, flour and other dried produce.

Order: Coleoptera
Family: Tenebrionidae
UK species: 37
World species: 15,000
Body length: 2–45 mm

Tenebrio obscurus

Snout Beetles or Weevils

The species of this gigantic family are by far the commonest insects on Earth. All weevils have a snout or 'rostrum' which carries the jaws. The family has members associated with almost every species of plant. Nearly all are herbivorous and they eat every bit of a plant, from root to seed. If disturbed, they usually lie still or fold their legs under their body and fall to the ground, playing dead. Many species like *Sitophilus granarius* (Grain Weevil, shown here), are serious pests.

Order: Coleoptera
Family: Curculionidae
UK species: 400
World species: 41,000
Body length: 1–50 mm

Jumping Bristletails

If you search under stones in grassy or wooded areas, in rock or leaf litter, or on rocks on the seashore above the high-tide line, you should be able to find some of these little bristletails. They look rather like silverfish (see page 74), but are brownish in colour and have a humped thorax. When you disturb them, they jump before making for cover. Hunt for them with a torch after dark because they are attracted to light. Shine the torch at one point on the ground for about 2–3 minutes and see what appears. They feed mainly on algae, mosses, lichens and decaying organic debris.

Petrobius maritimus is often found on rocks near the sea.

Order: Archaeognatha
Family: Machilidae
UK species: 7
World species: 250
Body length: Up to 12 mm

Leafhoppers

A massive family – it is thought that almost every plant species has at least one species of leafhopper eating it. All of them suck plant juices.

Graphocephala fennahi (the Redbanded Leafhopper, shown here) is found on rhododendrons. Female leafhoppers lay up to 300 eggs in the tissues of the host plant. The nymphs produce large amounts of honeydew which certain species, known as sharpshooters, can expel rapidly or spot on to leaves. Many species produce up to five distinct types of sounds. In this way they recognize their own species and find a mate. Many species are serious pests of crops and other important plants.

Graphocephala fennahi

Order: Hemiptera
Family: Cicadellidae
UK species: 262
World species: 21,000
Body length: 3–20 mm

Treehoppers

Many treehoppers have strange humps, spines and other projections from the back of the thorax. If you touch one gently, you will see it hop. Some species look very much like thorns, as does *Stictocephala bisonia* (American Buffalo Treehopper, shown here), and this disguise helps them to be unnoticed as part of a plant. This species is often found on apples, willow, hawthorn and lime. The nymphs of all species excrete honeydew and many are attended by ants who gather the sweet liquid. In return the ants guard the treehopper nymphs from attack. There is evidence of maternal care, as the females of many species guard the young nymphs from attack.

Order: Hemiptera
Family: Membracidae
UK species: 2
World species: 2,500
Body length: 5–13 mm

Common Earwigs

Species in this family are found in ground litter, soil, under loose bark or in rocky crevices. If you search in such places, you will soon find them – often dozens of individuals clustered together. In some species the female stands guard over her eggs. This is an example of primitive maternal care. She even licks the eggs to keep them free of infection. The forceps at the tail-end are used for courtship and defence. Despite their name, they are very unlikely to get into human ears. Some species are garden pests because they chew flower petals.

Order: Dermaptera
Family: Forficulidae
UK species: 3
World species: 465
Body length: Up to 35 mm

Forficla auricularia

True Crickets

These are found in all kinds of herbage in woodlands, scrub, meadows and grassland. Most species hide away under stones, logs or leaf litter. Others live in trees, while some live

The singing organs on the front wings consist of a row of pegs. The song is produced by the male rubbing these against the rear edge of his left forewing.

underground, but certain members of this family live in domestic situations. Some are active by day, others nocturnal. The species shown is *Acheta domesticus* (the House Cricket), which was once very common in old houses and bakeries. Today, due to increased cleanliness and modern building methods, they are not found so often.

Order: Orthoptera
Family: Gryllidae
UK species: 3
World species: 1,800
Body length: 4–45 mm

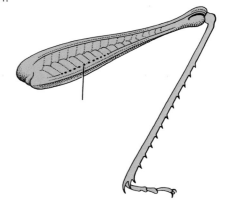

Tube-tailed Thrips

Members of this family are found in small habitats such as herbaceous plants, shrubs, trees, flowers, twigs and under bark. Some live in leaf litter and soil. Although this family contains some of the world's largest thrips, most are less than 4.5 mm long. While the majority feed on fungal threads and the spores of fungi, some are carnivorous.

Order: Thysanoptera
Family: Phlaeothripidae
UK species: 38
World species: 2,700
Body length: 1.5–4.5 mm

Haplothrips kurdjumovi

Common Thrips

Like the previous family, common thrips are tiny. If you look carefully among flowerheads, peas and beans and in the ears of cereals, you should find plenty of specimens. Despite their small size, they are important pests because they transmit virus diseases to many commercial crops. Sometimes these small insects are called thunderflies, because they seem to fly around just before thunderstorms.

Order: Thysanoptera
Family: Thripidae
UK species: 105
World species: 1,500
Body length: 0.7–2 mm

Limothrips cerealium (Grain Thrip) is a pest breeding in the ears of cereal crops. It is less than 2 mm long.

Brown Lacewings

Micromus angulatus

A family of carnivorous insects found in deciduous woodland, gardens and hedgerows. One brown lacewing may eat many thousands of aphids, mealy bugs and scale insects. They are therefore very effective in reducing natural populations of some pests. The best time to look for them is when they become active from dusk onwards. They produce several broods in a year.

Order: Neuroptera
Family: Hemerobiidae
UK species: 29
World species: 900
Body length: 4–12 mm

Common or Green Lacewings

Green Lacewings are very common and you should easily be able to find some. They sometimes come to lighted windows and are mainly nocturnal. You will find them in all types of vegetation, where their prey – aphids, scale insects and mites – live. Some species have incredible bat-detecting, ultrasonic sound receivers in the veins of their wings – a useful way to avoid being snatched out of the sky by a hungry bat. Green lacewings often hibernate in houses and attics.

Order: Neuroptera – Family: Chrysopidae
UK species: 14 – World species: 1,600
Body length: 10–25 mm

Chrysopa carnea has bright golden, brassy or reddish eyes, which seem to shine.

Common Sawflies

Sawflies are, of course, not flies at all. They are in the same insect order as wasps, ants and bees. Unlike those creatures, sawflies have no waist. Their name refers to the saw-like ovipositor (egg-laying tube) of the females. With it they cut slits in leaves, twigs or shoots of their host plants and lay their eggs there.

Order: Hymenoptera
Family:
Tenthredinidae
UK species: 400
World species: 4,000
Body length: 3–22 mm

Strongylogaster macula

Ants

You can find ants in every colour from pale yellow to black. They live in colonies and are adapted for their particular tasks. You will mostly see the wingless workers, but the queens, who lay the eggs and the males who fertilize them, have wings. Look for ants disappearing into holes in the ground in your garden. They also live in natural cavities and build nests above ground. Search in conifer woods for the great mounds of leaves and pine needles that are the home of Wood Ants.

Ants can be plant- or meat-eaters, or eat both foods. Many are addicted to the honeydew produced by aphids (see page 10) or the sap of plants. Some ants have powerful biting jaws. Others can sting you or spray formic acid, which stings.

Order: Hymenoptera
Family: Formicidae
UK species: 42
World species: 8,800
Body length: 1–20 mm

Lasius niger

Antlions

At a quick glance these large, slender-bodied insects look like damselflies (see page 56). But if you look more closely and carefully you will see that Antlions have club-ended antennae. They are only found in southern Europe, not in Great Britain. They are called antlions because some species prey on ants. The larvae live in sand at the bottom of conical pits. When an ant arrives, the antlion larva flicks sand at it. When the ant falls into the trap, it is seized and eaten.

Myrmeleon formicarius

Order: Neuroptera
Family: Myrmeleontidae
UK species: 0
World species: 1,000
Wing-span: 35–120 mm

Ladybirds

Ladybirds come in a variety of colours and number of spots. The background of the wing-case can be black, red, yellow or orange, and the number of spots can vary from two to twenty-four. They are found in a wide range of habitats, as long as suitable food is available. The adults of most species feed on aphids and soft-bodied insects. Their larvae also eat vast numbers of aphids (see page 10). In addition to their warning colours, ladybirds give out a yellow fluid from their leg joints, which makes them distasteful to predators.

Order: Coleoptera
Family: Coccinellidae
UK species: 41
World species: 5,000
Body length: 1–10 mm

Adalia bipunctata

Robber or Assassin Flies

A well-named family because their mouthparts are adapted for stabbing and sucking. Most species will perch on an exposed twig or stone where they keep a look-out for a passing insect. If one flies near, the assassin fly chases it and seizes it on the wing with its strong, bristly legs. It quickly injects a nerve anaesthetic which paralyses the prey. Some species hunt for ground-moving prey. Many of the family mimic bees and wasps, and no insect prey is too large for them. They catch and kill dragonflies, bees and grasshoppers, as well as other insects.

Order: Diptera Family: Asilidae
UK species: 27 World species: 5,000
Body length: 3–50 mm

Dioctria baumhaueri

Dance Flies

The common name of this predacious family comes from the mating swarms that occur in summer in which males fly up and down in a dancing fashion. They feed by catching small flies. Males sometimes offer prey items to females to eat while they mate with them. Some dance flies take prey from spiders' webs. Their habitat is moist places near water. Their larvae live in humus, leaf litter, decaying wood and vegetation, under bark and in water. They eat blackfly, scale insects and mites. Much remains to be discovered about these insects.

Order: Diptera
Family: Empidae
UK species: 350
World species: 3,500
Body length: 1.5–11 mm

Dolichocephala irrorata

Long-legged Flies

These flies will be found in wet habitats, such as marshy places, stream and lake margins, meadows and woodland. A few species live on the seashore. The adults seize small insects, which they crush and chew before sucking up the juices. Look for them during the summer months. A great deal remains to be discovered about many of their larval ways of life. In the way that birds use parts of their body to signal to mates, these flies do the same. The males have hairy tufts and other 'decoration' on their legs which they show off to females.

Order: Diptera
Family: Dolichopodidae
UK species: 270
World species: 5,500
Body length: 0.8–7 mm

Dolichopus ungulatus

Humpbacked or Scuttle Flies

With their humped backs these small flies scuttle about on compost heaps, rotting fungi and around the nests of rodents and ants. If you use your sweep net in such locations, you may find one scuttling among the assorted flies you have caught. They are quite small, but you should be able to find some where you live. As with all small insects, you need to observe closely and patiently. The larvae of some of these flies are internal parasites of other insects and a few are pests of cultivated mushrooms.

Order: Diptera
Family: Phoridae
UK species: 277
World species: 2,800
Body length: 0.6–6 mm

Megaselia pleuralis

Hover or Flower Flies

On any sunny day during the summer you can see hover flies doing aerial acrobatics. They can move suddenly in any direction, even backwards, or hover over a flower head. Look for them on flat-topped flower clusters as they feed on pollen and nectar. The slug-like larvae of many species eat thousands of aphids. Although they look like bees and wasps, they have no sting.

Order: Diptera
Family: Syrphidae
UK species: 245
World species: 6,000
Body length: 3–34 mm

Syrphus vitripennis **can hover like a tiny helicopter, even in wind and bad weather.**

Leaf-mining Flies

You are more likely to find the signs of their larvae than to see the adults, simply because these flies have no easy recognition features. The adults lay their eggs in plant tissue and the larvae make mines between the upper and lower leaf surfaces. If you search through the leaves of holly between September and May, you should be able to find the work of the Holly Leaf Miner. Try keeping some mined leaves in a sealed container (see page 73). You can see the adult flies, and some of their parasites, hatch.

Agromyza reptans

Order: Diptera – Family: Agromyzidae
UK species: 300 – World species: 2,500
Body length: 1–6 mm

House Flies

You have certainly seen one of these flies land on the window or your food, or noticed them walking upside-down on the ceiling. As they feed on decaying material and excrement, many of them spread diseases like cholera, typhoid fever and dysentery among human beings. The female lays eggs in masses on rotting plant or animal matter. In about a week they hatch into larvae, which are commonly known as maggots. While we may resent the habits of *Musca domestica* (House Fly, shown here), we should try to appreciate how perfectly they are adapted to their way of life.

Order: Diptera – Family: Muscidae
UK species: 275 – World species: 3,000
Body length: 2–12 mm

Blow Flies

Typical species of this family are the familiar bluebottle and greenbottle flies. You have most probably seen one when it flew indoors attracted to your food. Adults feed on flower pollen and nectar as well as rotting animal and plant matter. Being fond of carrion and dung makes them carriers of diseases such as dysentery. One species lays its eggs on the wool of sheep. The larvae then bore into the flesh of the sheep, leaving terrible wounds. Other species attack worms, and still others suck the blood of nestling birds.

Order: Diptera
Family: Calliphoridae
UK species: 33
World species: 1,200
Body length: 4–16 mm

Calliphora vomitoria

Found Almost Everywhere

White, Sulphur & Orange-tip Butterflies

Pieris rapae (Small White)

This family contains some of the world's most common butterflies. Their habitats range from woodlands to meadows and from mountains to sea level. Caterpillars of the best-known species feed on the cabbage family. In good summer weather Large Whites and Small Whites breed so fast that they become pests on cabbage crops. Others feed on alder, hawthorn and willows. Look for Orange Tips flying along hedges in early summer. Only the male Orange Tip Butterfly has orange-tipped wings. Search for the Sulphurs (also known as Brimstones) along hedges with some buckthorn bushes.

Order: Lepidoptera – Family: Pieridae – UK species: 10 World species: 1,300 – Wing-span: 20–70 mm

Blue, Copper & Hairstreak Butterflies

Lycaena phlaeas (Small Copper)

We do not know a lot about the life cycles of many of these brilliantly coloured, iridescent blue, copper or purplish butterflies. About one-third live in association with ants. The butterfly larvae produce a sugary fluid which the ants eat. In return the ants guard them. The caterpillars of some species even feed on the larvae in the ants nest. As many of this family are very beautiful, they have been over-collected and are close to extinction. Many are now protected by law.

Order: Lepidoptera – Family: Lycaenidae UK species: 18 – World species: 6,000 – Wing-span: 15–50 mm

Tortricid Moths

Species of this large family of smallish moths show many cryptic patterns on their wings. Some of the patterns make them look like bark, others resemble lichen, bird droppings and bits of leaves. They are found in a wide variety of habitats. There are many pest species in the family, notably *Cydia pomonella* (Codling Moth, shown here). The caterpillars of some species bore into stems and leaves, and a few cause galls.

**Order: Lepidoptera
Family: Tortricidae
UK species: 308
World species: 4,500
Wing-span: 8–34 mm**

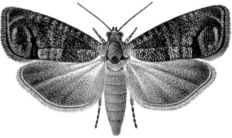

Pyralid, Snout & Grass Moths

The front wings of this family are usually oblong or triangular with closely packed scales. In some species the front of the head looks as if it has a small snout. This is the third largest family of moths, so there is a huge range of colour, shape and size in the different species. Many are pests: *Ostrinia nubilalis* (European Corn-borer, shown here) damages young corn when a caterpillar. Others attack maize (sweetcorn), sunflowers, apples, cabbage and other food crops.

**Order: Lepidoptera
Family: Pyralidae
UK species: 165
World species: 17,500
Wing-span: 10–40 mm**

Biston betularia

Geometrid Moths

The caterpillars of this enormous family move by a looping motion. They draw their hind end up to meet the front end in a loop, then push the front end forward. This gives them their family name, Geometridae, meaning earth-measuring. The adult moths can be found almost everywhere that plants grow, and in summer many will fly in and settle on lighted windows. Very many species are pests of trees and crops.

Order: Lepidoptera – Family: Geometridae
UK species: 270 – World species: 18,000
Wing-span: 14–42 mm

Hawkmoths

The moths in this family have swept-back wings, like the wings of a fighter plane. Many species visit garden and park flowers, such as petunias, at dusk. Elephant Hawkmoth caterpillars occasionally feed on fuchsia. The Privet Hawkmoth, as the name suggests, is found on garden and wild privet bushes. Hawkmoths' habitats cover a great variety of wooded and open areas, including gardens and parks, where their food – plants, trees and flowers – may grow.

Hyles lineata (Striped Hawkmoth)

Order: Lepidoptera
Family: Sphingidae
UK species: 18
World species: 1,200
Wing-span: 35–150 mm

Tiger & Ermine Moths

Tiger moths are mainly nocturnal, heavy-bodied, hairy and often brightly coloured. The bright colours warn their predators that they are don't taste good; some are even poisonous. The best time to search for *Arctia caja* (Garden Tiger Moth, shown here) is when it is on the wing in July and August.

Ermine moths tend to be pale or white with small black spots or patches. Due to the variety of their food plants, they are to be found in a wide variety of habitats. The caterpillars are covered with hairs that cause a rash in humans.

Order: Lepidoptera
Family: Arctiidae
UK species: 40
World species: 2,500
Wing-span: 20–70 mm

Noctuid Moths

Species from this enormous family of moths can be serious pests of crops of all kinds. With a medium-sized wing-span, mostly 20–45 mm, they are dull in colour with narrowish front wings. The antennae are hair-like in females, but brush-like in males, who often have a tuft of hairs at the end of the abdomen. They fly at night and are found in almost every kind of habitat. They have thoracic hearing organs which can detect and evade bats. *Agrotis ipsilon* (Dark Sword-grass Moth, shown here) is a common visitor to Britain.

Order: Lepidoptera
Family: Noctuidae
UK species: 350
World species: 25,000
Wing-span: 15–80 mm

Common, Paper & Potter Wasps

Being found in a wide range of habitats these are easy to recognize as 'real' wasps with their black with yellow or white markings. They are some of nature's most elegant architects. Their nests, where a queen, males and sterile female workers form a social colony, are made by the workers chewing up wood fibres or paper. They feed their larvae on chewed insects, which they capture alive. The adults feed on nectar and other sugar-rich foods.

Vespula germanica

Potter wasps do not live in colonies. They collect mud or clay and make vase-shaped nests underground or in plant stems. They then paralyse a caterpillar and suspend it from the roof as a form of preserved food for the larva.

Order: Hymenoptera – Family: Vespidae
UK species: 30 – World- species: 3,800
Body length: 8–25 mm

Solitary Hunting, Digger & Sand Wasps

The common names of these various sub-groups tell you their different habits. They live in sunny, sandy, open habitats. The adults feed at flowers and any source of sugary liquid. The females hunt and catch insects and spiders, which they paralyse or kill. The prey is placed in the nest, in the ground, rotten wood, hollow stems or burrows of other insects. Once the nest burrow is stocked with prey and eggs are laid, the larvae will develop on the food store.

Ectemnius cephalotes

Order: Hymenoptera – Family: Sphecidae
UK species: 115 – World species: 8,000

Plasterer & Yellow-faced Bees

Plasterer bees make simple nest burrows in the ground or in natural cavities in stones and bricks.

Yellow-faced bees nest in the pith of plant stems, the empty burrows of wood-boring insects, and plant galls. They do not have pollen baskets on their legs, instead they have to swallow the pollen in order to carry it to their nest. They then regurgitate it to provision the larval cells.

Hylaeus bisinuatus is a yellow-faced bee, although it doesn't have a yellow face.

Order: Hymenoptera – Family: Colletidae
UK species: 20 – World species: 3,000
Body length 3–18 mm

Mining or Andredid Bees

Look for these bees in any flower-filled habitat in spring and early summer. As early as March you will see them on dandelions, coltsfoot and sallow catkins. You may find tiny mounds of soil, signs of their burrow-building, on your lawn or in grassy, sunny banks. Although they are solitary bees, some species tend to make their burrows in large groups. They put pellets of mixed pollen and honey in their burrows as food for the larvae. Some species are parasitized by the well-named cuckoo bees (see opposite). These bees are common pollinators of spring flowers.

Order: Hymenoptera
Family: Andrenidae
UK species: 67
World species: 4,000
Body length: 4–20 mm

Andrena clarkella

Leaf-cutter & Mason Bees

Members of this large family of bees are common everywhere in areas where there is plenty of dead wood or pithy plant stems to provide nest sites. Most species are solitary. They collect mud, resin, leaf matter or plant hairs to line their larval cells. If you search carefully on rose bushes in parks or gardens during June and July, you may find almost circular holes cut into the leaves. This is the work of a leaf-cutter bee.

Mason bees dig their cells into mud beneath stones, on earth banks and occasionally in galls. Some species of this family are important pollinators of crops and other plants.

Order: Hymenoptera
Family: Megachilidae
UK species: 40
World species: 3,000
Body length: 7–21 mm

Megachile centuncularis

Halictid or Sweat Bees

Only some species are attracted to sweat in addition to the normal diet of pollen and nectar. The bees in this family will sting, but it is not very painful. Some species are solitary; others are semi-social. The female is long-lived and often guards her pollen-stored cells until the young bees emerge. Most make burrows in firm soil, such as garden paths, especially with clay or sandy soils.

Order: Hymenoptera
Family: Halictidae
UK species: 58
World species: 5,000
Body length: 4–15 mm

Halictus rubincundus

Digger, Cuckoo & Carpenter Bees

Anthophora furcata

Digger bees dig burrows, cuckoo bees lay eggs in the nests of other bees and carpenter bees excavate burrows in timber. Their habitat is widespread – they live wherever there are plenty of flowers. They are mainly solitary bees. Cuckoo bees leave their young to feed on pollen and honey collected by their host. Digger bees collect a supply of honey and pollen and leave it in the larval cells.

Order: Hymenoptera – Family: Anthophoridae
UK species: 43 – World species: 4,200
Body length: 3–28 mm

Bumble Bees & Honey Bees

Bumble Bees are those large, furry, buzzing bees that visit flowers throughout the summer. In sunny weather in March and April, watch for a large queen bumble that has just come out of winter hibernation. She will make a mossy nest on or under the ground. Her 300 or 400 eggs will first produce sterile worker bees to build up the colony and collect food.

Honey bees are much smaller and often start a colony in a hollow tree or roof space. They are also kept in hives by bee-keepers. A single queen may lay tens of thousands of eggs to produce workers, and up to 2,000 males or drones. Honey bees collect nectar and pollen from flowers. They store pollen and the honey they make in thousands of wax cells which make a comb.

Order: Hymenoptera
Family: Apidae
UK species: 27
World species: 1,000
Body length: 3–27 mm

Bombus lucorum

An Insect Safari

There are insects everywhere on Earth, from the frozen tundra plains to the jungles and deserts of the tropics. There are more than 1.5 million species of animals in the world, ranging from the primitive amoebas to humans. Of these species, over 932,000 are insects – or nearly two-thirds of all the known species. On every square kilometre of land, there will be thousands of millions of insects to be found.

Insect watching

A good time to study insects such as bees, wasps, dragonflies and butterflies is on a warm, sunny day when there is no wind. If you want to watch night-time (nocturnal) insects such as moths, a warm, still summer evening is best.

What to take

When you go looking for insects, it is a good idea to take these pieces of equipment with you:

1 **Hand lens**: helps you to look at small insects close up and in great detail. Buy a folding one that magnifies things 10 times (labelled x10) and wear it on a cord round your neck.
2. **Glass or plastic jars with holes bored in the lid:** useful if you find a large insect and want to put it somewhere safe while you look at it.
3 **A pooter:** see opposite for how to make one.
4 **A sweep net:** for trapping butterflies and moths temporarily.
5 **A beating tray or pale umbrella:** for investigating trees and bushes (see page 63).
6 **Field notebook with pencils and pens:** make notes of the date, the weather, where you go and what you find.
7 **Lightweight backpack:** this is the most comfortable way to carry your equipment and leaves your hands free.

Making a pooter

A pooter helps you to pick up and look at bugs and other small insects without harming them. It is quite easy to make a pooter of your own.

1 **Take a piece of clear plastic** 12 cm square and roll it into a tube. Secure it with some sticky tape.

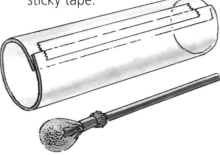

2 **You will also need two wide drinking straws** and a piece of gauze 6 cm square. Place the gauze over the end of one of the straws and tape it in position.

3 **Find some modelling clay or Blu-Tack** and make two round blobs, each about the size of a ping-pong ball. Squash them flat into disc shapes, then push a straw through the middle of each one.

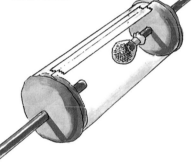

4 **Put one disk at each end of the plastic tube,** so that the gauze is inside the tube.

5 **When you suck at the straw with gauze on the other end,** air will rush into the plastic pooter through the other straw. If you then gently hold your pooter close to a bug and suck on the straw, the insect will be caught safely and quickly.

6 **Once you have finished looking,** release the insect by removing one end of the pooter. Always try to put insects back where you found them.

7 **Remember to use your pooter carefully,** and never try to catch spiders or large insects such as butterflies, as you could harm them.

Where to look

You probably don't need to look far on your insect safari to see a beetle on the ground or a bee at a flower. You can find other kinds of insects on leaves, plant stems, under stones and under loose tree bark. Spend some time watching the insects that you find to see where they go and what they do. If you look carefully, you will learn lots more about the way they live.

Look under leaves to find insects like shield bugs.

Look on plant stems to find insects like aphids and ladybirds.

Look under paving stones in your garden to find ants' nests.

Look under loose tree bark to find insects like earwigs.

Look under rotting logs to find insects like beetles.

Meadows & Fields

This habitat also includes hedgerows, heaths and roadsides – these are all grassy areas, rich in wild flowers. Flowering fields are great places to search, especially for butterflies and other flying insects feeding on nectar from the flower heads. Ancient meadows that have been left unploughed for many years are particularly good places to explore – many are now nature reserves.

You can think of hedges as a sort of scaled-down woodland with a rich undergrowth of plants. Hedges also form safety corridors for species to move from place to place. Scientists have proved that hedges and wild field margins are very important to agriculture because natural enemiesof insect pests, like parasitic wasps and predatory beetles, shelter here. There they can survive and combat crop pests when they appear in the fields.

The vast majority of hedges exist as borders to fields. The farm animals and crops in the fields attract many insects of all kinds. In hedges you should search for insects in the fallen leaf litter near the ground while others are to be seen flying in to feed on the flower nectar.

Heathland with its beautiful gorse and heather is a fast disappearing habitat in Britain today. Developers regard it as 'derelict land and ideal for development'. But as an insect hunter and watcher you will find a sunny heath swarming with life. This picture shows nine insects from this section; see how many you can identify.

Blister Beetle, Damsel Bug, Dung Fly, Ground Beetle, March Fly, Short-horned Grasshopper, Skipper butterfly, Soldier Beetle, Tumble Flower Beetle.

Tiger Beetles

Look for these beetles in sunny, warm open areas such as dry heaths and sandy places. Choose a sunny day in spring to early summer. Adult tiger beetles are fierce predators and are among the fastest insect runners. They have a top speed of 2.6 kilometres per hour. Their larvae dig vertical burrows, often 30 cm deep. They wait at the top, head and jaws filling the opening to seize any passing insect and drag it down to be eaten. Both larva and adult beetle thoroughly live up to their name of Tiger Beetle.

Cicindela hybrida

Order: Coleoptera – Family: Cincindellidae
UK species: 6 – World species: 2,000
Body length: 6–24 mm

Earth-boring Dung Beetles

As their name suggests these beetles are found beneath dung of all kinds, carrion and in decaying wood or fungi. The adults dig out burrows many centimetres deep and stock these tunnels with balls of dung. A single egg is laid on each ball. The larva feeds on the dung. Some species feed on plant material, but most of the family are valuable as scavengers and dung removers.

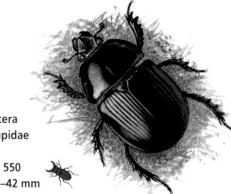

Order: Coleoptera
Family: Geotrupidae
UK species: 8
World species: 550
Body length: 5–42 mm

Geotrupes stercorarius (the Common Dor Beetle). The word 'dor' comes from an ancient word meaning 'drone' and refers to the humming flight of the beetle. It flies in the evening and is attracted to light.

Soldier Beetles

Some species of this family are very common, so you should quite easily find a few. Look, in warm sunshine, on flowers, along verges and the edge of woodland. They seem to be particularly fond of wild parsley flowers. Although the adults of some species eat pollen and nectar, adults and their larvae hunt for prey on the ground. The soldier beetle in the picture can be found on grass and nettles, especially if you search for it in early summer. Birds rarely attack them – this is probably because of the beetle's bright yellow, red or orange warning colours.

Order: Coleoptera
Family: Cantharidae
UK species: 41
World species: 4,000
Body length: 3–30 mm

Cantharis rustica

Fireflies or Lightning Beetles

A wonderful example of this family is *Lampyris noctiluca* (the Glow worm, shown here). The female has no wings and emits a bright green light on the end of her body. After dark its purpose is to attract flying males to come and mate. Each species has its own special flashing signal. The beetles are able to control the amount of oxygen supply to the special light organs, where a chemical reaction produces a cold, greenish light. They are not common, but you may find one glowing on a grassy bank or in a hedge. The larvae of many species feed on snails.

Order: Coleoptera
Family: Lampyridae
UK species: 2
World species: 2,000
Body length: 5–25 mm

Tumbling Flower Beetles

Look out for these beetles on flowers of the daisy family and flowers with flat tops like hogweed and cow parsley. In warm sun they may be found at rest on tree trunks. The reason for their common name is their habit of tumbling off their resting place when disturbed. Adults feed at flowers, but some of their larvae burrow in plant stems or live in decaying wood, while others bore inside fungi. Members of this family are not pests.

Order: Coleoptera
Family: Mordellidae
UK species: 10
World species: 1,250
Body length: 2–15 mm

Tomoxia biguttata

Order: Coleoptera
Family: Meloidea
UK species: 9
World species: 2,000
Body length: 5–35 mm

Meloe proscarabaeus

Oil or Blister Beetles

Beware! These beetles produce fluids which can raise blisters on your skin, so look but do not touch. You may see them on flowers and low-growing foliage. The larvae of many species are found in the soil and eat the eggs of grasshoppers or bees. In some species the larva attaches itself to the body of a solitary bee visiting a flower. When the female bee lays her eggs, the beetle larva sneaks into the cell with the egg. It then eats the bee's egg and the food provisions left by the parent bee for its intended offspring.

Meadows & Fields

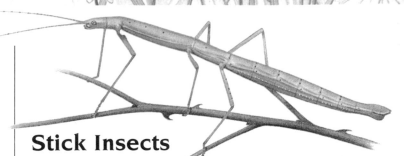

Praying Mantids

These insects hold their front legs in an attitude of prayer, which is how they got their name. But they are simply waiting to seize any passing insects with their spiked legs. They are probably the only insects that can look over their shoulders. Their habitat is almost anywhere that has a regular supply of insect prey. They are able to snatch flying insects out of the air. They are not found in Britain. If handled, they try to bite, but are not dangerous. A female lays a couple of hundred eggs, contained in an egg case called an 'ootheca' which is attached to a plant.

Order: Mantodea
Family: Mantidae
UK species: 0
World species: 1,400
Body length:
20–150 mm

This **Mantis religiosa (European Mantid) is waiting to seize a passing insect – with split-second timing.**

Delphacid Planthoppers

This family is common everywhere in grassland, meadows, pastures and woodland margins. Adults have sucking mouthparts to feed on plant sap. Although grasses and sedges are their main host plants, they also attack other plants. Some species have become serious crop pests; the Sugar-cane Leafhopper, for example, was accidentally introduced from Australia to Hawaii, where it caused terrible damage to sugar-canes. It was brought under control by using a small bug that ate the eggs of the leafhopper.

Order: Hemiptera – Family: Delphacidae
UK species: 70 – World species: 1,800
Body length: 2–9 mm

Javesella pellucida

Stick Insects

Their long legs and tubular green or brown body make these insects resemble twigs and sticks. In the wild they sway gently in a breeze to imitate the motion of the twig. If disturbed, they fall and lie still on the ground. They feed mostly by night and hide during the day. Their habitat is among grassy vegetation or in trees and shrubs. Stick insects can shed their legs if attacked, and regrow them during future moults. The *Carausius morosus* (Laboratory Stick Insect, shown here) grows up to 90mm long.

Order: Phasmatodea – Family: Phasmatidae
UK species: 0 – World species: 600 – Body length: 25–130 mm

Short-horned Grasshoppers & Locusts

Their common name describes their short antennae. They are found on the ground and on plants in meadows, hedges and many other similar places in summer time, and are plant eaters. If you walk slowly through a field on a sunny summer day, you will hear them chirping. They sing by rubbing a row of small pegs on the inside of their hind legs against the hard edge of the front wings. The Desert Locust, one of the most damaging pests in the world, belongs to this family.

Order: Orthoptera
Family: Acrididae
UK species: 11
World species: 9,000
Body length: 10–80 mm

Chorthippus brunneus (Field Grasshopper)

Damsel Bugs

These bugs are to be found in a wide range of habitats, from the ground to vegetation of all kinds, as long as small insects are available as prey. They catch and suck out aphids, caterpillars and many kinds of soft-bodied insects. You may find some by sweep-netting dry grassland such as hay fields. Do not handle roughly as members of this family can give you a painful bite. They are useful to humans because they help to control natural insect populations which include pest species.

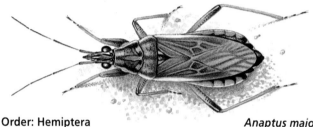

Anaptus major

Order: Hemiptera
Family: Nabidae
UK species: 13 – World species: 400
Body length: 3–12 mm

Scentless Plant Bugs

You may find members of this family on weeds and rank vegetation in old fields and other similar undisturbed habitats. A few live in trees, so look out for one when tree-beating. Like so many other bugs, they suck the juices of leaves, seeds and fruit of their host plants. The best time to look for them is late summer and early autumn. *Liorhyssus hyalinus* (Hyaline Grass Bug, shown here) varies from black to yellow. Its main food is daisies.

Order: Hemiptera
Family: Rhopalidae
UK species: 8 – World species: 150
Body length: 5–14 mm

Ground or Seed Bugs

These are usually to be found in leaf-litter, under stones or in low-growing vegetation such as stinging nettles. Most of the family are seed-eaters who use their strong and spined front legs to grasp their food. Some are plant-sap suckers and a few are predacious. They produce sounds which may help to attract a mate. They use well-developed scent glands to protect themselves against enemies. Many species are pests to garden and farm crops and cause great damage.

Kleidocerys resedae

Order: Hemiptera – Family: Lygaeidae
UK species: 75 – World species: 3,500
Body length: 2–18 mm

Burrowing Bugs

Burrowing bugs may be found under stones, dead leaves, decaying wood and around the base of weedy plants. All species are known to be able to burrow under ground. Eggs are laid in soil and their nymphs feed on root sap. Some species guard their eggs. Both sexes have pegs on the hind wings which can be rubbed against the body to produce sounds during courtship. The female *Sehirus bicolor* (Pied Shieldbug, shown here) guards her eggs for 3 weeks and turns them with her mouth parts.

Order: Hemiptera
Family: Cydnidae
UK species: 9
World species: 400
Body length: 2–10 mm

March Flies

These insects were originally called St Mark's flies because they are seen on the wing in swarms around 25 April, which is the feast day of St Mark. The females lay 200–300 eggs below ground, and their larvae eat all kinds of organic material and plant roots. Their habitats are gardens, flower-rich pastures and similar places. The picture shows *Bibio marci*, a typical member of the family. You may see one or more of these hairy-bodied flies flying slowly on a sunny April day with its legs dangling down.

Order: Diptera
Family: Bibionidae
UK species: 19
World species: 780
Body length: 5–11 mm

Soldier Flies

A family of robust, metallic-sheened flies favouring a damp habitat. Look for them sitting on flowers of willow, hawthorn, daisies and flowers with flat tops, like water hemlock. You may hear some flying with a wasp-like hum over marshy ground from June to August. The name Soldier Fly comes from their armour of spines on various body parts. Some of their larvae, living under bark, may control bark beetles (see page 43).

Sargius cuprarius

Order: Diptera
Family: Stratiomyidae
UK species: 50
World species: 1,800
Body length: 2–17 mm

Fruit Flies

Search for these quite beautiful flies around flowers and vegetation. You may be fortunate enough to watch their courtship behaviour. The males of many species walk to and fro in front of the females. As they do so they slowly wave one of their attractively patterned wings while holding the other upright. Many of their larvae live inside soft fruits, in the flowerheads of daisies and related plants, or as stem and leaf miners and gall formers. As pest species, some attack citrus fruits, peaches, cherries, apples, walnuts and melons. *Ceratitis capitata* (the Mediterranean Fruit Fly, shown here) is a very serious pest in subtropical and tropical regions.

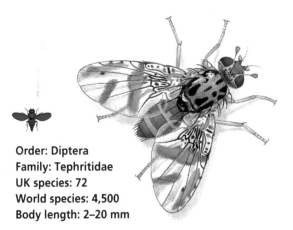

Order: Diptera
Family: Tephritidae
UK species: 72
World species: 4,500
Body length: 2–20 mm

Some species cause galls to form on thistles. You may find some if you search carefully. Each gall contains several growing larvae.

Black Scavenger or Ensign Flies

Members of this family are to be seen on flowers, vegetation and around dung or decaying plant and animal matter. Adult males display their wing tips by walking to and fro and flicking their wings outwards. This is done to attract females. When you are watching an insect, look for interesting behaviour. Make notes in your field notebook when you observe something (see page 24).

Order: Diptera
Family: Sepsidae
UK species: 26
World species: 250
Body length: 2–6 mm

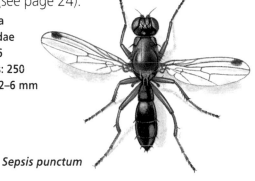

Sepsis punctum

Stem, Grass or Frit Flies

Their habitat is grassy meadows and among rank vegetation, flowers and decaying organic matter. The adults of this family eat nectar, prey on root aphids or eat the eggs of spiders, moths and other insects. A few, however, are important pests of farm crops. The larvae of most species are herbivorous. Those of *Oscinella frit* (shown here) damage cereal ears by boring into them.

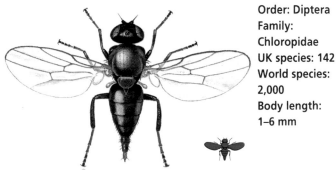

Order: Diptera
Family: Chloropidae
UK species: 142
World species: 2,000
Body length: 1–6 mm

Dung Flies

You are most likely to encounter these flies around pasture land and farms where cattle are kept. They are best avoided because they carry disease germs on their feet. Not all the family lay eggs in dung. Some, in complete contrast, are laid in orchids and lilies. Adult dung flies are all predacious on small insects. It is perhaps a little odd that the family are called dung flies when many are not associated with dung. While the habits of many flies may seem unpleasant to us, their way of life helps to recycle materials back into the ecosystem.

Order: Diptera
Family: Scathophagidae
UK species: 53
World species: 250
Body length: 3–13 mm

Scathopaga stercoraria
Yellow Dung Fly

Anthomyiid Flies

This is a very large family of rather ordinary-looking flies, which somewhat resemble house flies. Their adult food varies, ranging from pollen and nectar to small insects. Some of their larvae may be found as stem-borers, gall-formers and leaf-miners, while others live in rotting seaweed or bird droppings. A few species of *Delia* damage onions, turnips, cabbage, wheat and carnations, and have become serious pests. Since they are so common, it should not be too long before you see one.

Order: Diptera
Family: Anthomyiidae
UK species: 225
World species: 1,500
Body length: 2–12 mm

Delia platura

Meadows & Fields

Swallowtail & Apollo Butterflies

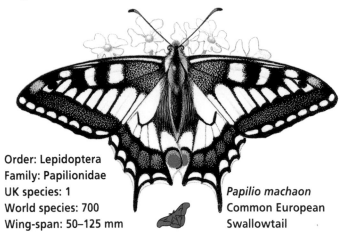

Order: Lepidoptera
Family: Papilionidae
UK species: 1
World species: 700
Wing-span: 50–125 mm

Papilio machaon
Common European
Swallowtail

This family includes the very large bird-wing butterflies of southeast Asia, the largest butterflies in the world. Swallowtails and apollos are perhaps the loveliest of all butterflies. They are beautifully marked with yellow, orange, red, green or blue. To see a swallowtail in Britain, you will have to go to the Norfolk Broads. Their caterpillars feed on many plants, including milk parsley, angelica, fennel and wild carrot.

Apollo butterflies do not have hind wing tails and are white or grey in colour. They are found in high Alpine meadows in Europe. Many of these families are protected by the law in parts of the world. However, it is even more important to protect their habitats or they will become extinct.

Milkweed Butterflies

The name 'milkweed' refers to the food-plant of this butterfly's caterpillars. You would be extremely fortunate to see one of this family in Britain. However, *Danaus plexippus* (American Monarch Butterfly, shown here) does occasionally reach British and European shores. It is an amazing migration for so delicate a creature, but they regularly travel from Canada to California and Mexico, where vast numbers assemble and roost. Their bright colours are a warning that they taste nasty, so birds leave them alone as a result.

Order: Lepidoptera
Family: Danaidae
UK species: 1
World species: 300
Wing-span: 60–100 mm

Skippers

This family name refers to their active, rapid and darting flight patterns – they almost 'skip' from flower to flower. You will find them in habitats where their caterpillars' food-plants grow. Although these are mainly grasses, some species like the Dingy Skipper, are found on Birdsfoot Trefoil and other plants. Unlike other butterfly caterpillars, this family lives within a shelter of silk-tied or rolled leaves. The caterpillars pupate at the plant's base within a silken web. You should search for skippers on a sunny day in meadows, rough grasslands, downs and woods.

Thymelicus lineola
European Skipper

Order: Lepidoptera
Family: Hesperiidae
UK species: 8
World species: 3,500
Wing-span: 20–65 mm

Stem Sawflies

Like all sawflies, the females in this family have an ovipositor (egg layer), which is modified as a saw. They literally saw into plant stems to make a slit in which to lay their eggs. Their larvae look very much like the caterpillars of moths or butterflies, and burrow inside the stems of grasses, willows and other plants. Unlike other sawfly larvae, their legs are very small indeed. Look for the slow-flying adults around yellow flowers. *Cephus pygmaeus* (Wheat Stem Sawfly, shown here) is a pest of cereal crops. Although it looks a little like a wasp, a closer look will reveal that it has no 'waist'.

Order: Hymenoptera
Family: Cephidae

UK species: 12
World species: 100
Body length: 4–18 mm

Velvet Ants

Another misleading common name – these insects are velvety, but although some of them look like ants, they are not ants. The males of some species are found on flowers. The females are wingless and are usually seen running over the ground in dry, shady or open habitats. They are parasites on the larvae and pupae of many bees and wasps. Female velvet ants have incredibly powerful stings which cause intense pain – so don't pick them up.

Order: Hymenoptera – Family: Mutillidae
UK species: 3
World species: 5,000
Body length: 3–25 mm

Mutilla europaea concentrates on bumble bees as food for their larvae.

Spider-hunting Wasps

Adults can be seen on flowers or running over the ground in open, dry, sandy habitats. They flick and jerk their wings continuously as they run. Their venom will paralyse even the largest spider, but the wasp has to avoid the spider's venomous fangs. If successful, the wasp lays a single egg on the paralysed spider and buries it in the sand. A few species cheat by laying an egg on another wasp's prey. Either way, the growing larva has spider-meat for a meal. Beware these wasps; their stings are extremely painful.

Order: Hymenoptera
Family: Pompilidae
UK species: 41
World species: 4,000
Body length: 5–55 mm

Anoplius nigerrimus

Tiphiid Wasps

Adults of this family feed on flower nectar and honeydew. Females are usually seen running over the ground. All are parasitic on the larvae of beetles, bees and wasps. The ant-like female of *Methocha* will run over the ground searching for tiger beetle larvae (see page 28) in their burrows. She has to avoid the larva's powerful jaws, paralyse it and lay her egg. She then fills in the burrow. *Tiphia* species (shown here) parasitize the larvae of dung beetles (see page 28) and cockchafers (see page 76). Some species have been investigated as possible biological control agents.

Order: Hymenoptera
Family: Tiphiidae
UK species: 3
World species: 1,500
Body length: 4–30 mm

Attracting Insects

A garden makes a very good nature reserve for insects. Even in the smallest town garden you can find hundreds of different kinds. A garden contains plenty of things for insects to feed on, and lots of places to hide. See how many different insects you can see in your garden. If you enjoy watching them it is easy to encourage even more to visit your garden or window box.

Insect favourites

Butterflies, bees, and other flying insects visit flowers to feed on their sweet nectar. Buddleia, thistles, and other purple flowers are especially popular. In fact buddleia is such a favourite with butterflies such as Red Admirals that it is nicknamed the "Butterfly bush".

A wild corner

Why not ask if you can leave a small area of the garden to grow wild? You could also scatter some wild flower seeds in your wild patch. You can buy packets of wild flower seeds at your local garden centre. Don't dig up wild plants from the wild.

The wild plants that will grow there will encourage all sorts of interesting insects to move in. Nettles provide food for caterpillars, while dandelions, daisies, and buttercups attract bees and butterflies by offering them nectar to sip. In return the insects help the flowers to reproduce.

Bees' homes

To attract solitary bees to your garden, you could make some bee nesting burrows, using a tin can, some large drinking straws, and a piece of wire.

1 **Find a clean, empty tin can and a handful of large drinking straws.** If the straws are longer than the can, ask an adult to cut off the ends so that they are all 2 cm shorter than the tin. This will keep the rain out.

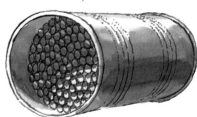

2 **Fill the can with enough straws** so that they cannot move around inside.

Moth feast

You can encourage night-time insects such as moths by making them a tasty feast. All you will need is some brown sugar, some mushy, overripe bananas or pears, a little brown beer, a mixing bowl, and a paintbrush.

1 **Put 500 gm of brown sugar** into a mixing bowl and add one or two mushy bananas or pears. Add a little brown beer and stir the mixture well.

2 **At dusk go into the garden** with your mixture and a paintbrush. Paint some strips about 5 cm wide and half a metre long on to the bark of a few trees.

3 **Wait patiently** for your hungry visitors to arrive.

4 **Take a small torch** with you. It will help you to watch the insects when it gets dark.

3 **Take the piece of wire and wind it** around the middle of the can. Fasten it so that you have enough wire left to hang the can up.

Making a pond

One of the most interesting ways to attract dragonflies is to make a pond. This is quite simple to do, and it also makes a perfect water habitat for water boatmen and water beetles.

1 **Decide where you want to put the pond**. Check with an adult before making a final decision.
2 **Ask an adult to help you dig a hollow** about half a metre deep, using a garden spade.
3 **Buy a sheet of plastic pond lining** from your local garden centre. It must be big enough to fill the hollow and spread out over the edge of the pond by a few centimetres.

4 **Now ask an adult to help you fix the bee home** under the roof of the garden shed or on a fence post.
5 **Watch from a distance.** In a few days you should see some bees making their nests inside. Remember bees can sting you!
6 **To make an even simpler bee home,** find a rotten log and ask an adult to drill lots of holes in it for you. Place the log on a wall or fix it to the shed, and wait for the bees to arrive.

4 **Put some soil in the bottom of the pond** and around the edges, to cover the top of the plastic lining and keep it in position.
5 **To plant your pond,** you will need one or two pond plants in pots, and some pond weed (like Water Milfoil). Ask your garden centre for advice on what to plant.

Make a mini pond

If you don't have a garden, or if your garden is too small for a pond, why not make a mini pond? Simply fill an old washing-up bowl with water and a few small water plants, then wait and see what happens.

6 **Secure the plant pots with stones** so that they don't move about, then fill the pond with water.
7 **It may take several months,** or even a year before insects begin to appear in your pond, but it's worth being patient. However, you may see mosquito and midge larvae within a few days.

Woodlands

This habitat includes forests, woods, their margins and clearings within them. Forests are very large areas dominated by trees which can be coniferous (trees with needles), deciduous (trees that lose their leaves in autumn, like oaks or chestnuts), or a mixture of both.

Woodlands are often small patches left over from the ancient forest that once existed in that area. The environment inside a wood or forest is sheltered from winds and is cool and humid. In winter it stays fairly frost-free and all kinds of wildlife can find shelter among the trees throughout the year. Deciduous woods in spring, before the trees grow leaves, may have lots of flowers. You will find bees and many other insects visiting these flowers for pollen and nectar.

Mature woods and forests with lots of different trees and with sunny clearings are the very best places for you to find insects. You should search for them in every part of a tree; the leaves, roots, bark, wood, flowers, fruit and so on. Did you know, for instance, that an average oak tree provides a living and home for more than 300 animal species? The majority of these are insects.

As you explore a wood, look out especially for strange growths on leaves, buds and bark. These are formed by gall wasps. Search through leaf litter as well and you will find many other specialised insects. This picture shows nine insects from this section; see how many you can identify.

Conifer Sawfly, Gall Wasp, Horntail, Horse Fly, Lappet Moth, Longhorn Beetle, Long-horned Grasshopper, Common Scorpionfly, Stag Beetle.

Woodlands

Long-horned Grasshoppers & Bush-crickets

Members of this family can be found from ground level to the tree tops. They are active between dusk and dawn, when you may hear the males 'singing'. You can recognize a female by its deep and sickle-shaped ovipositor. *Metrioptera roeselli* (Roesel's Bush-cricket, shown here) likes damp, luxuriant vegetation. It can be found on southern coastal marshes in Britain. In summer you may find crickets in hedgerows and after harvest in corn fields. Smaller ones may be found in your beating tray (see pages 62–63) from oak or lime trees.

Order: Orthoptera
Family: Tettigoniidae
UK species: 6
World species: 5,000
Body length: 15–75 mm

Subterranean or Damp-wood Termites

Species of this family are found only in warmer regions. There is one species of termite in Europe, and none in Britain. Their nests are found in damp soil or damp timbers, and they are pests because they feed on wood and can thus damage buildings. They are social insects, living in huge colonies. They are divided into workers and soldiers, each with separate functions. Despite the damage they cause, they are vital in the recycling of nutrients and an important link in ecosystems.

Order: Isoptera
Family: Rhinotermitidae
UK species: 0
World species: 200
Body length: 5–8 mm

Reticulitermes flavipes

Narrow Barklice

These are small, soft-bodied insects whose habitat is the underside of leaves, twigs and branches of deciduous trees. Many prefer holly, box and rhododendron. They lay their eggs in groups of 5–10 on stems, leaves and fruit. These eggs are sometimes parasitized by fairyflies (see page 68). It seems incredible to think that a minute wasp less than 2 mm long is able to find tiny eggs laid by a fly less than 5 mm long.

Order: Psocoptera
Family: Stenopsocidae
UK species: 3
World species: 45
Body length: 1–5 mm

Graphopsocus cruciatus

Common Barklice

If you want to find these little insects, you will have to search very thoroughly on and beneath the bark of trees, and also on twigs and branches. If you are lucky, you may encounter a herd of many hundreds, even thousands, on tree bark. They glue their eggs into crevices in the bark and cover them with a crusty layer or even silk. There are many species still awaiting discovery.

Order: Psocoptera
Family: Psocidae
UK species: 12
World species: 500
Body length: 1–6 mm

Trichadenotecnum variegatum

Cicadas

The bugs in this family are well known for their songs, which are easy to hear. Each species has its own song. The songs are produced by a pair of drum-like organs called 'tymbals', one each side of the body near the thorax. A muscle is attached to the tymbal. Each time it contracts or relaxes, a series of sharp clicks is produced. The muscle contracts and relaxes very rapidly to make the song. The nymphs live underground, moult many times and may take from four to seventeen years to become adults because of their poor diet of root sap. There is one rare and local British cicada known as the New Forest Cicada.

Order: Hemiptera – Family: Cicadidae
UK species: – World species: 2,500
Body length: 23–55 mm

Magicicada septemdecim
Periodic Cicada

Froghoppers

Adult froghoppers are active jumpers, like the spittle bugs (see pages 10). Their habitat is meadows, scrub and woodland, all with plenty of vegetation. Their nymphs suck sap from plant stems, which produces a frothy foam. This protects them from some predators and also prevents evaporation. *Cercopis vulnerata* (shown here) is a good example of the warning colours which tell any enemy it is dangerous to eat. Many species are pests and can damage plants by their feeding activities.

Order: Hemiptera
Family: Cercopidae
UK species: 1
World species: 1,400
Body length: 5–20 mm

Lace Bugs

These small bugs are really beautiful. To appreciate the lace-like patterns you will have to take a close-up look with your hand-lens. Their habitat is the underside of leaves, especially the foliage of trees and flowers in the garden border. Other species live on creeping thistles and rhododendrons. A few species are attended by ants while others make gall on their host plant. The females of some species guard their eggs, recognize their own young and even shepherd the young nymphs from leaf to leaf.

Order: Hemiptera
Family: Tingidae
UK species: 23
World species: 1,820
Body length: 2–5 mm

Dictyonota fuliginosa

Snakeflies

Their English name comes from the way they resemble a snake when they hold their heads up. The long 'neck' is a feature of these insects, which are to be found from May to July in thickly wooded areas. The females have a long, thin ovipositor, which is easy to see. This is used to place eggs into openings in bark, and their larvae live under loose bark. Both adults and larvae are predators on aphids (see page 10) and other small, soft-bodied insects.

Order: Megaloptera
Family: Raphidiidae
UK species: 4
World species: 85
Body length: 6–28 mm

Raphidia xanthostigma

Woodlands

American Cockroaches

Many of these large, fast-running cockroaches are brown or reddish-brown with a shiny appearance. Their oval, flattened bodies let them hide behind skirting boards and in narrow crevices. Their legs are spiny. When running about they continually wave their antennae to and fro. They are found both in the wild and in buildings; they were accidentally introduced into Europe with ship's cargoes. A female *Periplaneta americana* (American Cockroach, shown here) may lay up to fifty egg cases, which look like tiny purses – each contains 12–14 eggs. Some species of these nocturnal insects emit a foul-smelling liquid.

Order: Blattodea
Family: Blattidae
UK species: 3
World species: 600
Body length: 25–45 mm

Stag Beetles

The common name of these large shiny, black or reddish-brown insects refers to the huge jaws of the male, which look a bit like antlers. They are used for fighting during courtship. Their habitat is wooded areas or along sandy beaches. Look for them from May to July on tree trunks, fences and even pavements, especially in southern England. They fly by night. The larvae live for up to four years in decaying tree stumps.

Order: Coleoptera – Family: Lucanidae
UK species: 3 – World species: 1,250
Body length: 6–85 mm

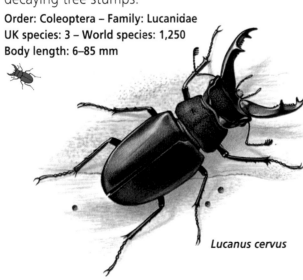

Lucanus cervus

Jewel Beetles

This family includes many of the most beautiful beetles in the world. They look a little like Click Beetles (see page 76), but do not 'jump'. They are found in coniferous and deciduous woods. Female jewel beetles lay eggs in wood, and the larvae chew tunnels in roots and trunks of trees. Some species are leaf-miners, and some bore into plant stems. Biologists have evidence that these beetles possess infra-red detectors to locate burned areas where some lay their eggs. They react to disturbance by flying off or pretending to be dead.

Melanophila acuminata

Order: Coleoptera
Family: Buprestidae
UK species: 12
World species: 14,000
Body length: 2–65 mm

Pleasing Fungus Beetles

These small to medium-sized oval and shiny beetles have a metallic sheen. Where tree bark is damaged and sap is flowing down the trunk, they move in to a rich source of food. Most lay eggs on fungi and the larvae burrow deep within to feed on the fruiting bodies of the larger fungi. If you come across some fungus-infected, rotting wood, look a little closer – there may be some of this family about. Some species feed on bracket fungi, which usually grow on wood. They are a good example of how insects have adapted to a wide variety of food sources.

Order: Coleoptera
Family: Erotylidae
UK species: 7
World species: 2,000
Body length: 3–25 mm

Dacne bipustulata

Longhorn Beetles

Search for these attractive beetles, sometimes called timber beetles, on flowers in a variety of habitats. Nocturnal species hide during the day under litter debris or bark. Many species are cryptically coloured and others display warning colours to warn off predators. Most of them have long, narrow bodies. Their antennae are long, mostly two-thirds to four times as long as the body. Their larvae burrow into timber. Some have been known to emerge from furniture made from attacked timber.

Saperda populnea

Order: Coleoptera
Family: Cerambycidae
UK species: 60
World species: 25,000
Body length:
3–130 mm

Bark Beetles

Members of this family are found in close association with many coniferous and deciduous tree species. Bark beetles have been responsible for changing the appearance of the countryside. The larvae of some species spread Dutch Elm Disease by carrying a fungus infection which clogs the sap channels of the tree and kills it. You may find the signs of these beetles if you peel back the bark of fallen or dead trees (see page 49). Many species produce chemical attraction odours called 'pheromones'; these attract many other beetles and so cause a huge infection of the tree.

Polygraphus poligraphus

Order: Coleoptera – Family: Scolytidae
UK species: 54 – World species: 9,000
Body length: 1–8 mm

Furniture & Deathwatch Beetles

These are small, hairy, light brown or black beetles. Most measure about 2–6 mm. Some species produce larvae which bore into wood and so are known as woodworms. Their habitat is all kinds of wooden structures, either indoors or outside. The adult of some species attracts a mate by tapping its head against the walls of the tunnel inside the timber. These faint sounds can be heard in a quiet room. Others attack stored tobacco, spices and drugs. *Anobium punctatum* (Furniture Beetle, shown here) is present in many old houses.

Order: Coleoptera
Family: Anobiidae
UK species: 28
World species: 1,500
Body length: 1–8 mm

Woodlands

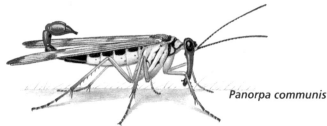

Panorpa communis

Common Scorpionflies

Their common name is obvious if you look at the end of the male's abdomen, which looks almost exactly like a scorpion's sting. Actually, it is the part of the male's reproductive system that engages with the female during mating. The head has a beak-like extension which is armed with biting mouthparts used to seize and eat dead or dying insects. Some species rob spider webs of freshly caught prey. Look for these insects on low-growing vegetation in shady places such as woodland margins.

Order: Mecoptera – Family: Panorpidae
UK species: 3 – World species: 360
Body length: 9–25 mm

Moth & Sand Flies

The habitats of both families are damp, shaded places like bogs and woods. The larval form of many species is unknown, and many other psychodid species remain undescribed. Some moth flies, which are sometimes called owl midges (subfamily: Psychodinae), are nocturnal and are attracted to lights. You may find some on your windows in spring and summer. Adult moth flies do not bite.

Sand flies (subfamily: Phlebotominae) feed on the blood of humans and many other vertebrates. They also carry unpleasant diseases. However, there are no sand flies in Britain.

Order: Diptera – Family: Psychodidae
UK species: 76 – World species: 1,000
Body length: 1.5–5 mm

Psychoda alternata

Fungus Gnats

These are mosquito-like flies favouring moist, woody areas, but they are also found in houses. Look for the long legs and humped thorax, like the adult *Mycetophila fungorum* (shown here), and adults on the wing between March and August. The worm-like, whitish larvae of some species feed in dung, rotting wood and other plant matter. Others feed on woody bracket fungi or fleshy fungi. A few live in caves and emit a light to lure other small insects into silken threads.
Various species are a serious pest to cultivated mushrooms.

Order: Diptera
Family:
Mycetophilidae
UK species: 420
World species: 3,000
Body length: 2–13 mm

Horntails or Wood Wasps

The spine or horn at the rear of the body gives this family its common name. Below this spine the female has a long ovipositor which drills through the tree's bark and then a single egg is laid. The female *Urocerus gigas* (shown here) drills into the bark of conifers, especially firs and pines, to lay her eggs. Development may take two or more years. Males are much less easy to find and normally fly much higher in the tree canopies. If you see a horntail, do not be alarmed – it does not sting.

Order: Hymenoptera
Family: Siricidae
UK species: 11
World species: 100
Body length: 20–40 mm

Heleomyzids

They prefer shady, moist places, like thickets and overgrown woodland, but some have been found in mammal burrows, bird's nests and bat caves. Their larvae generally feed on decaying plants, dung, animal corpses, fungi and seaweeds. *Heleomyza serrata* (shown here) is a typical species. Little is known about the biology of many species in the family.

Order: Diptera
Family: Heleomyzidae
UK species: 60
World species: 500
Body length: 2–10 mm

Tabanus bovinus

Horse Flies

Species of this family are also known as gad flies, clegs, stouts and deer flies. The large, flattened head and large eyes are distinctive. The adult blood-sucking females will be found around mammals. They approach their prey with great stealth and alight on hard-to-reach places. Using their blade-like mouthparts, they cut into the skin and feed on the blood. The males can be seen feeding on flower nectar. The eggs are laid on plants and trees near water. The bite of these flies can cause painful swellings and even allergic reactions.

Order: Diptera – Family: Tabanidae
UK species: 28 – World species: 4,100
Body length: 6–28 mm

Conifer Sawflies

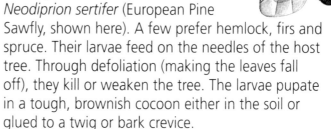

As in all sawflies, the ovipositor (egg-laying tube) in this family has evolved into a saw. With this the female cuts slits in leaves or stems and there lays her eggs. Conifer sawflies are found in conifer woods and plantations. Most species attack pine trees, like *Neodiprion sertifer* (European Pine Sawfly, shown here). A few prefer hemlock, firs and spruce. Their larvae feed on the needles of the host tree. Through defoliation (making the leaves fall off), they kill or weaken the tree. The larvae pupate in a tough, brownish cocoon either in the soil or glued to a twig or bark crevice.

Order: Hymenoptera – Family: Diprionidae
UK species: 7 – World species: 100
Body length: 5–15 mm

Gall Wasps

These small wasps lay their eggs inside plant tissue, then the plant produces an unusual growth called a gall. The larvae feed and grow within the gall, which protects and nourishes them. If you search in September along a hedgerow for wild roses, you will see one of the most attractive galls caused by *Diplolepis rosae* (shown here). The gall, called a Robin's Pincushion, is like a fluffy ball of red moss. Another place to look is on the foliage and stems of oak trees. There you will find oak-apple galls – they are easier to find than the tiny wasps.

Order: Hymenoptera
Family: Cynipidae
UK species: 95
World species: 1,250
Body length: 1–9 mm

Woodlands

Zeuzera pyrina
(Leopard Moth)

Carpenter or Goat Moths

The name Goat Moth comes from the fact that the larvae of some species leave a strong and sometimes unpleasant odour. These moths live in broad-leaf forests, and their larvae are found on oak, poplar, chestnut and willow trees. The adult lays her eggs on the bark and the larvae feed internally in the wood. Fully-grown larvae pupate in their tunnels or in the earth in a cocoon made of silk and chewed wood fibres.

Order: Lepidoptera – Family: Cossidae
UK species: 3 – World species: 1,000
Wing-span: 20–75 mm

Casebearing or Sac Moths

The caterpillars of this family feed on a range of trees, shrubs and plants in woodlands and damp meadows. As they grow, each makes itself a case from bits of its host plant, held together with silk. The adult moths lay their eggs in summer and the caterpillars spend the winter inside their cases. Several species are pests on apple and other fruit trees, birch, larch and other commercial trees, like the *Coleophora serratella* (Cigar Casebearer, shown here).

Order: Lepidoptera
Family: Coleophoridae
UK species: 101
World species: 800
Wing-span: 7–15 mm

Oecophorid Moths

Most of these moths can be found in a variety of wooded and open habitats. A very few species are to be found indoors. Not much is known about how their caterpillars behave, but some eat plants or fungus feeders, and others may feed on decaying matter.

Order: Lepidoptera
Family:
Oecophoridae
UK species: 80
World species: 3,500
Wing-span: 8–29 mm

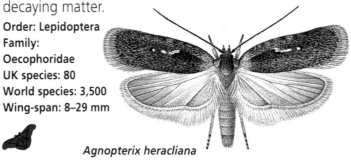

Agnopterix heracliana

Leaf Blotch-mining Moths

The caterpillars of these leaf-mining moths find a home between the upper and lower surfaces of leaves. In this small space they feed on the leaf tissue and so enlarge the space to form winding galleries or blotch-like patches. Search for their 'tracks' in leaves. You may discover *Caloptilia stigmatella* (Common Lilac Leaf-miner, shown here) in a garden, and some species are very common on oak trees. Look also for leaves which have the edges rolled; inside this rainproof tent you may find some caterpillars of the family. The adults fly at dawn and dusk and rest by day on tree trunks.

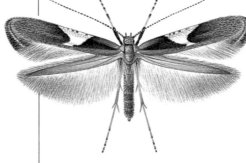

Order: Lepidoptera
Family: Gracillariidae
UK species: 80
World species: 1,200
Wing-span: 4–22 mm

Lappet & Eggar Moths

In general, this family chooses a woodland, hedgerow or heathland habitat. Be careful how you handle caterpillars of this family because their hairs can cause skin irritation. Some live communally in silk tents or webs spun over foliage. The fully grown caterpillars spin tough, papery, egg-shaped cocoons. You may find some of these moths flying at night, although many fly by day.

Malacosoma neustria (the European Lackey Moth) feeds on hawthorn and blackthorn trees.

Order: Lepidoptera – Family: Lasiocampidae
UK species: 11 – World species: 1,500
Wing-span: Up to 100 mm

Tussock Moths

These beautifully marked moths have no proboscis, so they do not feed. Both adults and their caterpillars have body hairs that can give you a severe skin rash. The caterpillars drop these irritating hairs all over their pupae to protect them. They are found in hedgerows, conifer and broad-leaf woodland, and hop fields.
Lymantria dispar (the Gypsy Moth, shown here) and the Brown-Tail Moth are two serious pest species on many trees.

Order: Lepidoptera
Family: Lymantriidae
UK species: 10
World species: 2,600
Wing-span: 20–60 mm

Arctic, Nymph, Ringlet & Satyr Butterflies

This is a family of shade-lovers found in heathland, open meadows and light woodland in upland areas. Their caterpillars all eat grass or sedges, and have a pair of points at the tail end. When on the wing these butterflies may be recognized by their erratic and bobbing flight. Common British species are found in shaded woodlands, fields, roadsides and gardens. The picture shows *Coenonympha tullia* (Large Heath Butterfly).

Order: Lepidoptera
Family: Satyridae
UK species: 11
World species: 2,000
Wing-span: 28–74 mm

Admiral, Emperor, Fritillary & Tortoiseshell Butterflies

A family of beautiful and colourful butterflies, most of which are common. Every sunny day you can see them flying and visiting flowers to drink the nectar. They are found everywhere – in meadows, woodland clearings and gardens. Their caterpillars are generally spiny and feed on nettles, thistles, sunflowers and other plants. Look among stinging nettles in July and August and you should find their larvae. Members of this family, like *Cynthia cardui* (Painted Lady, shown here), undertake migrations, and some species hibernate.

Order: Lepidoptera
Family: Nymphalidae
UK species: 18
World species: 3,500
Wing-span: 30–110 mm

Be an Insect Detective

Once you know where to look for insects, you can become an expert by exploring different habitats. Start by looking closely at a small habitat (a microhabitat), such as a pond, a compost heap, or even a window box, to see what lives there.

Looking at leaves and stems

Garden plants often contain evidence of all kinds of insect activity. Have a look in your garden to see what you can detect on the leaves and stems.

- Look carefully on a **blackberry bush** and you will probably find that some of the leaves are rolled up. Can you see a caterpillar inside?

- Little white lines on a **blackberry leaf** may have been caused by insects called Leaf-mining Flies (see page 19). Hold a leaf up to the light, or hold a torch behind it to see if you can detect the insects tunnelling through it.

- If you look closely at the leaves on a **rose bush** you will probably find that some have been nibbled around the edges. This is a sign that a Leaf-cutter Bee (see page 23) has been taking away pieces of leaf to make cocoons for its eggs.

- If the **stems and buds of roses** are sticky and green, this is probably a mass of Aphids (see page 10) which suck the sap inside the plant. You may also see a Ladybird (see page 17) feeding on the aphids.

- **Froth on the stems of a plant** is evidence of a Leafhopper (see page 14), which lives inside the bubbles that is known as 'cuckoo spit'. See if you can find some in your garden or park.

- **Swellings on grass stems or leaves** may contain the larvae of flies or moths. They are called 'galls'. Take some home and ask an adult to open them carefully with a sharp knife. Sometimes they contain a spider, ant or thrip which has moved into the empty gall.

Fungi homes

Fungi provide homes and food for many kinds of insects. If you look at the gills of a fully-grown wild mushroom, you may see little black specks. Look closer with a magnifying glass and you will discover that each speck is the head of a little white larva. Break open the mushroom to see how the larvae burrow tiny tunnels as they eat their way through it. Always wash your hands after touching fungi.

A world in an oak tree

A tree like an oak is a habitat for thousands of creatures. The leaves, fruits, and seeds are food for beetles, ants, aphids, bees, wasps, moths, and many more insects, which in turn are eaten by birds and mammals. Count how many kinds of insects you see buzzing around or crawling over a single tree. You may be surprised to discover that the tree is alive with wildlife. Make a note of the insects that you see and what they were doing.

Life inside a log

All kinds of creatures burrow into rotting wood and tree bark. If you find a piece of mossy, rotting wood, take it home in a plastic container. Keep the lid on so that the insects do not escape before you have finished studying them in their home.

1 **Peel away some moss and bark** to see what is hiding there. You may find beetles, earwigs, or even a centipede. Centipedes are not insects – they have too many legs – but they often hunt small insects.

2 **Break off part of the log** or piece of wood to see if there are burrowing insects. Holes in the wood may be woodworm, which is caused by burrowing beetle larvae.

3 **When you have finished** looking at your log habitat, put it outside in the garden.

Rivers, Lakes & Bogs

This habitat includes anywhere wet from marshes via ponds and streams to the seashore and salt marshes. The brackish pools in salt marshes have many bugs and beetles above the high tidemark. A few aphid species survive by feeding on sap from some of the plants which grow in the salty mud.

Freshwater is in short supply on the Earth's surface (ninety-seven per cent of the world's water is salt), yet it provides an amazing range of micro or macro-habitats for insects. There is a whole world to explore in a discarded jar or car tyre which may hold tiny 'pools' of rainwater. Such places are ideal breeding haunts for midges, mosquitoes and other flies whose larvae are aquatic. Hollows in trees, tree-holes and plant leaves that trap water at their bases also provide breeding sites.

In fast-running streams the only insects that can survive are those which have developed devices and modifications for holding on to the bottom. Slow-flowing streams, however, will have lots of interesting insects. Being shallow, streams have oxygen-rich water and nutrients which have run off the land via rainwater. Unfortunately farm chemicals, like pesticides, herbicides and fertilisers, also run off and can cause serious pollution.

Ponds have still waters which many insects like. A pond can grow a lot of algae when polluted by nitrate fertilisers. This can cause it to dry up – then everything dies. The picture shows eleven insects from this section; see how many you can identify.

Alderfly, Large Caddisfly, Narrow-winged Damselfly, Diving Beetle, Grouse Locust, Flatheaded Mayfly, Mosquito, Mole Cricket, Rolled-winged Stonefly, Water Boatman, Water Strider.

Rivers, Lakes & Bogs

Groundhoppers & Grouse or Pygmy Locusts

Reasonably common in some areas, their habitat is moist woodlands and the margins of bogs and lakes. They eat grasses, mosses and lichens. Unlike many species in this order, their courtship is silent. The male bows in front of the female and vibrates his wings. Members of this family do not stridulate (make the typical cricket sound) and have no hearing organs. Many species have grey or brown camouflage to match the mossy or stony ground where they live. There is still a great deal to be learned about their lifestyles.

Order: Orthoptera
Family: Tetrigidae
UK species: 3
World species: 1,000
Body length: 6–18 mm

Tetrix subulata
(Slender Grasshopper)

Mole Crickets

These generally reddish-brown insects show superb adaptations to subterranean life (under the soil). The front legs are modified for digging. Their eyes are small and their wings are leathery, covering only half the abdomen.From the front, they do look very like tiny moles. They live in sand or soil near streams, ponds or lakes, and their burrows can go 20 cm below ground. They build elaborate singing burrows with a special shape, which increases the volume of their song. On a still night they can be heard up to one kilometre away.

Order: Orthoptera – Family: Gryllotalpidae
UK species: 1World species: 60
Body length: 20–45 mm

Gryllotalpa gryllotalpa
(European Mole Cricket)

Striped Earwigs

Search for these nocturnal earwigs under debris, especially on seashores, mud flats and the banks of rivers, but you will be lucky to find one because they are not very common. *Labidura riparia* (Giant or Tawny Earwig, shown here) prefers sandy habitats where it can dig deep tunnels in which to lay its eggs. Handle these earwigs gently because they can give you a pinch with their tail-end forceps. They might also discharge a smelly liquid and some species can fire it over a short distance.

Order: Dermaptera
Family: Labiduridae
UK species: 1
World species: 75
Body length: Up to 35 mm

Mosquitoes

You will often hear these flies before you see them, for you can tell a flying mosquito by its high-pitched whine. Although the males feed on nectar and honeydew, the females are blood-suckers. When a female alights, she feels for a soft spot on the skin, then bores through it with her mouthparts and has her meal. You should look for the egg rafts of mosquitoes floating on the surface of water butts and other rain-filled containers and ponds. Their larvae, called 'wrigglers', hatch from these eggs. Put some in a jam jar and look at them with a hand lens, then return them to the place where you found them. In tropical countries mosquitoes are carriers of many diseases, including malaria and yellow fever.

Order: Diptera – Family: Culicidae
UK species: 36
World species 3,100
Body length: 3–9 mm

Culex pipiens

Non-biting Midges

This is a family of gnat-like flies that look a little like mosquitoes. Look for them between April and September over trees, bushes or water. You will often see swarms of them towards dusk 'dancing' up and down in still air, and the females mating before they lay eggs on the water surface. Most of their three-year life cycle is spent under water as larvae – the adults only live a week or two. The larvae of some species of this family are often called blood worms because of their red colour.

Order: Diptera
Family: Chironomidae
UK species: 400
World species: 5,000
Body length: 1–9 mm

*Chironomus
plumosus*

Biting Midges

Because of their small size midges are often called 'no-see-ums'. But you will certainly feel the effect of their biting and blood sucking, especially near sunset. They do not fly more than 100 metres from their breeding ground in moist habitats such as bogs, pond margins, rivers, lakes and close to the seashore. Large areas of Scotland remain unspoilt because of the bogs where some of the family live. Some species, like *Forcipomyia bipunctata* (shown here), suck the body fluids of larger insects.

Order: Diptera
Family: Ceratopogonidae
UK species: 165
World species: 2,000
Body length: 1–6 mm, mostly around 3 mm

Black Flies

The females of some species of this family require a blood meal from birds, horses and cattle before they lay their eggs. They have a stout body and a distinctive humpbacked thorax. The males suck nectar. Their habitat is around fast-flowing water, where the eggs are laid on plants or stones both above and below water. The larvae feed by filtering tiny particles and organisms from the water. In cool parts of the northern hemisphere they do not harm humans. However, in Africa they transmit river blindness and other parasitic diseases to humans, birds and animals.

Order: Diptera
Family: Simuliidae
UK species: 37
World species: 1,500
Body length: 1–5 mm, mostly under 4 mm

Simulium austeni

Shore Flies

This family is to be found in many types of wetland, such as marshes, wet meadows, pool margins, lakes, rivers and the seashore. Their larvae are either semi-aquatic or aquatic. They feed on sewage and carrion; some mine into meadow grasses and others live in the stems of water plants. While most shore flies prefer fresh water, some can tolerate very salty water. One unusual species can breed in pools of crude oil – a most unlikely habitat! A few of these flies have front legs like those of praying mantids (see page 30), which they use to capture small insects.

Order: Diptera
Family: Ephydridae
UK species: 130
World species: 1,400
Body length: 2–11 mm

Psilopa compta

Rivers, Lakes & Bogs

The Ephemeroptera are the oldest group of winged insects on earth today. The name of the order comes from two Greek words: *ephemeros* (lasting a day) and *pteron* (a wing) because the adults mostly live only a few hours.

Small Mayflies

To find the nymphs (young stages) of these beautiful mayflies, try pond-dipping in their habitat, which is still or running water. Streams, rivers, ditches, ponds or lakes may provide you with some specimens. If you keep some in your aquarium, be sure to plant it with a variety of aquatic plants because the nymphs are herbivorous (plant-eating). *Cloeon dipterum* (shown here) gives birth to live nymphs and does not lay eggs. Other species of small mayflies will enter water or even go through waterfalls to lay their eggs on rocks. Some species can live in polluted water, which is unusual for most insects.

Order: Ephemeroptera
Family: Baetidae
UK species: 14
World species: 800
Body length: 3–12 mm, mostly 4–7 mm

Burrowing Mayflies

Look for the adult Mayflies from mid-April to September when you may see vast numbers flying above a river or stream. The front legs of their nymphs are adapted for digging. They burrow into sand or silt at the bottom of streams, rivers, lakes or ponds. Their specially adapted mouthparts move the silt, which is then pushed backwards by the legs. Members of this family are important links in the freshwater-fish food chains. *Ephemera danica* (shown here) is the largest British burrowing mayfly. Anglers use models of it as lures, and it is known as a 'green drake'.

Order: Ephemeroptera
Family: Ephemeridae
UK species: 3
World species: 150
Body length: 10–32 mm

Flatheaded or Stream Mayflies

Try pond-dipping (see page 63) for the nymphs of these mayflies in fast-running mountain streams. If you catch one, observe it in some water in a plastic dish, then return it to its habitat. They are difficult to keep in an aquarium because they are used to cold, fast-running water rich in oxygen. As they are an important freshwater fish food, anglers use models of both nymphs and adults for fly fishing. They call the imitation pre-adult stage a 'dun' and the adult a 'spinner'.

Order: Ephemeroptera
Family: Heptageniidae
UK species: 11
World species: 550
Body length: 4–15 mm

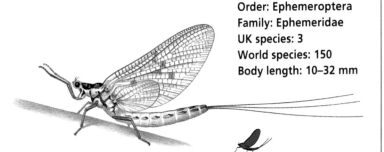

Rhithrogena semicolorata

54

Prongill Mayflies

One way to distinguish members of this family from other mayflies is by the length of their three long tails. In prongill mayflies they are obviously longer than the body. Their habitat is slow-flowing streams and lakes. The nymphs prefer to live in crevices under stones and logs, or in debris. They eat plants and detritus. These nymphs are freely eaten by fish and thus form an important link in the underwater food chain. Like many mayflies, the adults are used as models for fishermen's lures or 'flies'.

Leptophlebia marginata

Order: Ephemeroptera
Family: Leptophlebiidae
UK species: 6 – World species: 600
Body length: 4–14 mm, mostly 8–10 mm

Shore Bugs

As their name suggests, shore bugs are to be found around the margins of the seashore among seaweed, salt marshes, grasses, mosses and low vegetation. These species can survive being submerged by the tide. Many, however, may be found by streams, ponds, ditches and similar places. You will discover they are difficult to catch, as they hide away in holes and rock crevices. These bugs can run, jump and fly or burrow into mud, where some spend part of their life cycle. As far as is known, all members of this family are predacious (they hunt other creatures for food).

Order: Hemiptera
Family: Saldidae
UK species: 22
World species: 300
Body length: 3–7 mm

Saldula pallipes

Stilt Bugs

These bugs get their names from the way they walk with their bodies held high on spindly legs. Slow-moving, they 'freeze' if disturbed. Because of their secretive habits they are difficult to find. Their habitat is among tall grasses and weeds in woodlands, meadows and by the margins of ponds. The picture of *Berytinus minor* shows how their protective colouring helps them to merge into their surroundings. Although most are exclusively herbivores (plant-eaters), some species can be partly predators, feeding on insect eggs and small, soft-bodied prey.

Order: Hemiptera
Family: Berytidae
UK species: 9
World species: 180
Body length: 5–9 mm

Narrow-winged Damselflies

You will find this family mainly along streams and rivers, but also around ponds, brackish pools and swampy places. Damselflies are mostly smaller than dragonflies and have a feeble and fluttering flight. When at rest, the wings of damselflies are held together along the body, whereas in dragonflies they are held out sideways. Female narrow-winged damselflies use their ovipositors to make slits in submerged vegetation and then insert their eggs. In some cases, the female will crawl down under the surface to a depth of 30 cm or more.

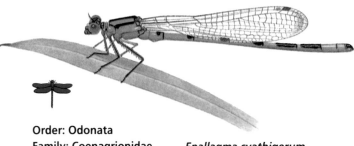

Order: Odonata
Family: Coenagrionidae
UK species: 12
World species: 1,000
Wingspan: 20–45 mm

Enallagma cyathigerum
(Common Blue Damselfly)

Spread-winged or Stalk-winged Damselflies

These relatively large damselflies are usually metallic blue, bronze or green in colour. Unlike members of other damselfly families, they rest with their wings slightly open and the body held vertical to the stem. On a warm, bright day between July and September you will see them sunning themselves on plants around still water, boggy areas, wet ditches or lakes. Females lay their eggs in plant stems above water level. Larvae take about eight weeks to develop. Like all dragonfly and damselfly larvae, they have a so-called 'mask' which is a part of the jaw folded back under the head. They lie in wait for a small fish or other aquatic life to come near, then the mask shoots forward and their strong claws seize the prey.

Order: Odonata
Family: Lestidae
UK species: 2
World species: 200
Wingspan: 32–64 mm

Lestes dryas
(Scarce Emerald Damselfly)

Hawkers & Darners

This family includes same of the largest and most powerful of the world's dragonflies. As the name hawker suggests, they hunt on the wing and seize many kinds of insects. Search for them in areas of still water during the midsummer months. They are inquisitive insects and investigate any moving object in their territory, including you. The aquatic nymphs, like all dragonfly nymphs, are aggressive. You can catch them in your pond net if you push it through pond vegetation (see page 63).

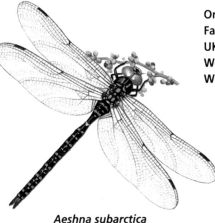

Order: Odonata
Family: Aeshnidae
UK species: 8
World species: 500
Wingspan: 55–110 mm

Aeshna subarctica

Common Skimmers & Darters

You will see these broad-bodied dragonflies flying over still water in a variety of habitats from dense forest to arid areas. Adult males are very territorial and will guard their patch from a high perch on an exposed stem or twig and chase off any intruder. Eggs are laid by the female hovering over the water and dipping the tip of her abdomen below the surface. The species shown here is often found in coastal areas, but can also be found in high hilly regions.

Order: Odonata
Family: Libellulidae
UK species: 13
World species: 1,250
Wingspan: 20–100 mm

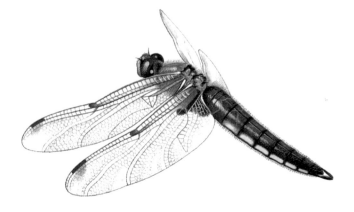

Libellula quadrimaculata **(the Four-spot Chaser) is a common migratory species**

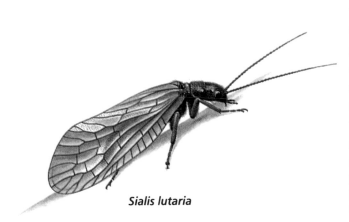

Sialis lutaria

Alderflies

If you search for these in May and June, you will find them at rest on alder trees and similar waterside vegetation. They are lazy fliers, so you should be able to take a close look at one without disturbing it. A female may lay many hundreds of eggs in clusters on waterside plants. The young larvae crawl into the water and live there for nearly two years. When fully grown, the larvae crawl out of the water and pupate on the land.

Order: Megaloptera
Family: Sialidae
UK species: 2
World species: 75
Body length: 10–20 mm, mostly under l5 mm

Spring or Brown Stoneflies

Nymphs may pass through thirty moults and take four years to become adults. Their eggs may be adhesive, flattened, spindle-shaped and with a thread-like attachment to stick to underwater objects. You should search for them in fast-flowing rocky streams. They are weak fliers, usually in warm sunshine. Many species avoid polluted water and prefer cold, oxygen-rich water. This family are used as models for the anglers' flies called 'Early Brown'.

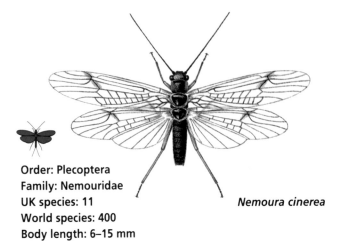

Order: Plecoptera
Family: Nemouridae
UK species: 11
World species: 400
Body length: 6–15 mm

Nemoura cinerea

Rolled-winged Stoneflies

Some species of this family are called needleflies because of their small size and slender shape. When at rest the wings appear to be tightly rolled together over the sides of the body. Their favoured habitat is small streams and springs, but they are also to be found beside lakes in lowlands and uplands. *Leuctra geniculata* (shown here) belongs to the largest genus in this family, which is found right around the northern hemisphere.

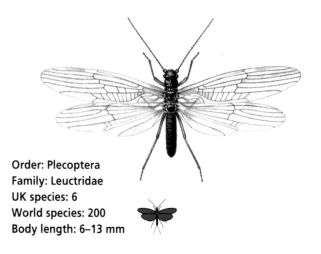

Order: Plecoptera
Family: Leuctridae
UK species: 6
World species: 200
Body length: 6–13 mm

Predatory Stoneflies

Some adult species of this family have no working mouthparts and live for less than two weeks using the food reserves within their bodies. Other species may feed on pollen. In contrast, their nymphs are carnivorous (meat-eating) or omnivorous (eat everything). When fully grown they crawl out of the water, rest on a stone and the adult emerges. They are found near cold, stony and gravel-bottomed streams; some species live in water rich in limestone. The best time to look for the day-flying adults is from late spring to early summer.

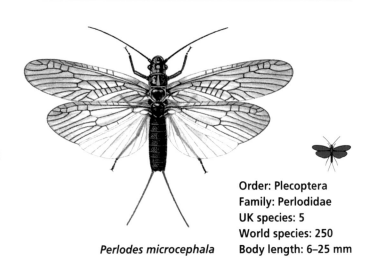

Perlodes microcephala

Order: Plecoptera
Family: Perlodidae
UK species: 5
World species: 250
Body length: 6–25 mm

Purse, Casemaker or Micro Caddisflies

The smallest species of caddisflies belong to this family. Their habitat is near rivers, lakes and ponds. Mating swarms fly over the water and lay jelly-like egg masses both on the water and marginal plants. The first four larval stages move freely in the water, sucking the juices of water plants. The last larval stage produces silk from its mouthparts and weaves an open-ended barrel or purse-shaped case. The larva pupates inside this case and emerges at the water surface.

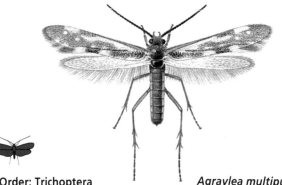

Order: Trichoptera
Family: Hydroptilidae
UK species: 29
World species: 1,000
Body length: 2–6 mm

Agraylea multipunctata

Northern Caddisflies

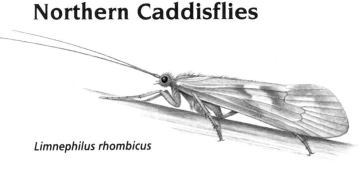

Limnephilus rhombicus

Search for these common caddisflies around ponds, lakes and still water. There are many species and their larvae live in cases made from tiny pieces of plant stem, stones, sand grains and small snail shells. Some species make cases from small twigs and these are known as log cabins. Use your pond net gently and push it through the underwater plants to catch the larvae.

Order: Trichoptera
Family: Limnephilidae
UK species: 54
World species: 1,500
Body length:
7–30 mm

A case made of tiny shells by the larva of a caddisfly.

Giant Casemakers or Large Caddisflies

Adults' wings of some species can be brightly marked with orange and black. You will find them near ponds, lakes, marshes and slow-moving parts of streams and rivers. The larvae make beautiful, regular, tapering cases of spirally arranged plant fragments. The pieces of plant fragment used are cut to an exact size as the larva measures them against the front part of its body. Some cases can be up to 60 mm long.

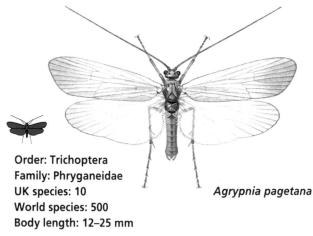

Order: Trichoptera
Family: Phryganeidae
UK species: 10
World species: 500
Body length: 12–25 mm

Agrypnia pagetana

Rivers, Lakes & Bogs

Water Striders or Pond Skaters

In this family the feet and underside of the body have a dense covering of water-repellent hairs. This enables them literally to walk on the water's surface. Their legs also have ripple-sensitive hairs, so if you tap the water's surface, you will see them react. Look for these interesting insects on still or slow-running water. Most species have winged, short-winged and wingless forms. The ones with wings can fly off to new sites and start new populations.

Order: Hemiptera
Family: Gerridae
UK species: 9
World species: 500
Body length: 2–19 mm, mostly 10–15 mm

Gerris gibbifer

Water Measurers or Marsh Treaders

This is a family of reddish to dark brown very slender bugs, which at first glance look a little like stick insects (see page 30). They are found on quiet pools, marshes, swamps, stagnant and even brackish water. Their bodies and legs are well covered with a pile of fine hairs which repel water. They walk slowly on the surface near the water's edge. They skewer small insect larvae and other small water creatures on their tube-like mouthparts.

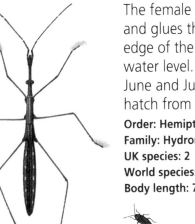

The female lays her eggs singly and glues them to plants at the edge of the water or to objects at water level. Search for them in June and July when new adults hatch from the eggs.

Order: Hemiptera
Family: Hydrometridae
UK species: 2
World species: 110
Body length: 7–15 mm

Hydrometra stagnorum

Backswimmers

Although they look a little like Water Boatmen, the backswimmers – as their name suggests – swim on their backs. Their long hind legs are fringed with hairs and used as oars. Strong swimmers, they can leap into the air through the surface film and fly away. At rest they hang from the surface. They are underwater predators feeding on insects, small fish, tadpoles – and even fingers if given the chance! Males can make sounds to attract females by rasping their mouthparts on their front legs.

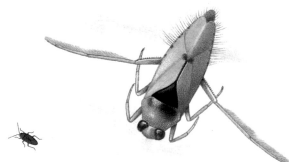

Order: Hemiptera
Family: Notonectidae
UK species: 4
World species: 300
Body length: 2–17 mm

Notonecta glauca

Water Boatmen

These are interesting insects, which can swim rapidly and which carry their air supply as a bubble in a reservoir under their wings. This makes them buoyant, so they have to hang on to plants in order to remain in deeper water. Some species are predacious on other aquatic insects and even fish Some species are unique among bugs because they can eat minute particles of solid food. All other bugs (order Hemiptera) suck up liquid food.

Order: Hemiptera
Family: Corixidae
UK species: 34
World species: 525
Body length: 3–15 mm

Glaenocorisa propinqua

Water Scorpions

Water scorpions lie in wait, hidden among vegetation, to ambush their prey. Their powerful front legs (known as raptorial legs) seize tadpoles, mosquito larvae and most other small water creatures. Having seized their prey, they suck out the body juices. They thrust their long breathing tube out through the surface film to renew their air supply. Although they are fully winged, they seldom fly. You might be lucky and catch them if you push your pond net slowly through the water weeds in slow-moving or still water.

Nepa cinerea

Order: Hemiptera
Family: Nepidae
UK species: 2
World species: 200
Body length: 15–45 mm

Diving Beetles

Most diving beetles carry a supply of air enclosed in their wing cases. They renew it by projecting their tail end into the air. Their habitats vary from streams, ditches, canals and lakes to ponds. If the habitat dries up, the beetles fly away to a new site. Both adults and larvae are predators on small fish, frogs, newts, snails and many other kinds of water life. They suck out the body contents after injecting a digestive substance into their prey. When you go pond-dipping (see page 63), you will almost certainly capture some.

Colymbetes fuscus

Order: Coleoptera – Family: Dytiscidae
UK species: 110 – World species: 3,500
Body length: 2–34 mm, mostly 5–25 mm

Whirligig Beetles

Look for groups of these beetles on the surface of slow-moving water and ponds. If you gently tap the water surface, you will see them react by diving because their antennae are sensitive to ripples. Although adapted for water life, they can fly well. Their blue-black, highly polished and streamlined upper body surfaces are waterproof. They use their two hind pairs of legs as oars and the front pair to seize mosquito larvae and dead insects floating on the surface. Search for these beetles at any time of the year although some may hibernate when it is very cold.

Order: Coleoptera
Family: Gyrinidae
UK species: 12
World species: 750   *Gyrinus minutus*
Body length: 3–16 mm

Catching Insects

If you want to look at water insects in your pond, or insects that you cannot catch with a pooter (see page 25), why not make some simple traps for collecting live insects without harming them?

Remember to handle all insects gently while you observe them, then set them free where you found them afterwards. Be extra careful not to trap insects that could sting you, such as wasps, bees, and hornets, and never try to catch delicate insects such as butterflies, moths, or dragonflies.

Make a beating tray

An easy way to look at insects that live on trees is to make a beating tray. **You will need**: two bamboo canes about half a metre long, one bamboo cane 1 metre long, some white cloth (a piece of old sheet will do), strong glue or a stapler, some string or wire, and a long stick.

1 **Place one of the short canes across the top of the long cane** to make a "T" shape, and secure it tightly with some string or wire.
2 **Then lay the other short cane across the middle** of the long cane, and fix it with wire or string so that it cannot move around.

Make a pitfall trap

The best way to catch crawling insects like beetles is to make a pitfall trap, which you put in the ground. **You will need:** a clean jam jar; a trowel; a large, flat stone and four pebbles.

1 **Choose a sheltered area of the garden** and dig a small hole in the earth, just deep enough for the jam jar.
2 **Put the jar into the hole** so that the rim is level with the ground. Make sure it doesn't wobble too much. Put a couple of leaves or a bit of grass into the jar.
3 **Put the flat stone over the top of the jar**, propped up by the pebbles to keep out the rain.
4 **Every few hours, remove the stone** and look to see if any beetles or other crawling insects have fallen into the trap. Have a look at night and in the early morning too.
5 **Remember that once an insect falls into the jar**, it cannot get out by itself, so you will have to release it.
6 **When you have finished using your pitfall trap**, remove the jar, and fill in the hole.

3 **Now cut enough white cloth** to lay across the bamboo frame and overlap the edges by 5 cm all round.

4 **Lay the cloth on the ground,** then lay the frame on top. Fold the edges of the cloth over the frame and fix it with fabric glue or staples. If this is difficult, ask an adult to help you. If you glue it, don't use the tray until the glue is dry.

5 **Now find a long stick, and a suitable tree** – oaks, beeches, or birches are good. Stand under the tree, holding your beating tray horizontally.

6 **Give one of the leafy branches a sharp blow**. Lots of different insects should drop on to your beating tray. You may find it easier if one person holds the tray and the other uses the stick. Be careful not to damage the tree.

Looking at water insects

Only ever visit a pond or stream with an adult, and approach quietly and carefully so that you don't disturb the water creatures. Never run, because you could easily trip and fall in.

If you want to catch pond creatures you will need a net. You can buy one quite cheaply, or you could make your own, using a bamboo cane with an old sieve attached to one end. You also need a bucket filled with pond water.

1 **Push your net slowly through the water,** close to the edges and around the plants.

2 **Lift the net out of the water gently,** then empty it by dipping it into the bucket of water.

3 **Don't forget to put the insects back** into the pond after you have identified them.

Pests & Parasites

These include insects which are pests of humans, their artifacts, buildings, livestock and crops. A lot is known about parasites and the insect pests whose attacks cause commercial damage. But the enemies of the vast majority of insect species are, as yet, unknown.

Parasites are those insects that eat the living tissues of their host or prey. They do not necessarily kill their hosts, although many do. In general an insect parasite uses one host animal in, or on, which to carry out its complete development from egg to adult. The eggs may be laid on or in the host, and the hatching larvae feed on the host's body tissues or fluids. If they do this on the host's outside (like bed bugs), they are called "ectoparasites'. If they do it from within the host, they are called 'endoparasites'. Many animals, for example birds, have their own specialised insect parasites – (louse flies, fleas, feather lice, etc) – while others live in birds' nests.

Houses have species that may 'live on the premises' or may come in for a short stay through an open door or window. Food stores and warehouses attract a variety of insects which may become pests, simply because there are such quantities of the food they like to eat.

Most insect pests attack a specific crop. They can range from the annoying, like black fly on a rose tree, to life-threatening, like the plagues of locusts that sweep across Africa eating everything in their path. This picture shows nine insects from this section; see how many you can identify.

Bean Weevil, Body Louse, Encyrtid Wasp, House Fly (see page 19), Ichneumon Wasp, Larder Beetle, Mealy Bug, Silverfish, Whitefly.

Parasites

Bird Lice

This family of tiny, wingless, parasitic lice have special claws adapted to hold on to their host's feathers. *Menopon gallinae* (Shaft Louse, shown here) gives you a good idea of a typical family member. You are more likely to see their effects than to find the lice unless you look very closely. The female attaches eggs singly to feathers by a waterproof, glue-like substance. The larvae then feed by scraping off the skin and feathers, which causes the bird to lose feathers in places and also become unhealthy.

Order: Phthiraptera
Family: Menoponidae
UK species: 146
World species: 650
Body length:
1–6 mm

Body Lice

The eggs of this small family are commonly known as 'nits'. The adults have curved legs, each armed with a large claw for grasping hair. There is one species who lives on humans but there are two distinct sub-species: the Body Louse and *Pediculus humanis* (Head Louse, shown here). The former lives in clothing, laying its eggs along the seams, but leaves to feed on human blood before hiding again. It carries typhus and other fevers. The Head Louse lives entirely in the hair and passes from host to host by the exchange of headgear, combs, brushes and direct contact.

Order: Phthiraptera
Family: Pediculidae
UK species: 1
World species: 2
Body length:
1.5–3.5 mm

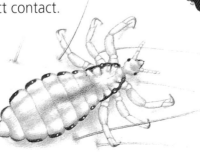

Mammal-chewing Lice

These small lice live in the micro-habitat provided by the hair or fur of their host mammal. Since they are always in very close contact with their host within a very small micro-habitat, they do not need sight, so they have evolved as eyeless or almost eyeless insects. Some, like *Trichodectes canis* (Dog Louse, shown here) are pests on domestic animals. This particular louse often transmits tapeworms from dog to dog. As they feed on skin, hair, fur and blood, they cause great irritation to their hosts.

Order: Phthiraptera
Family: Trichodectidae
UK species: 21
World species: 350
Body length: 1–3 mm

Common Fleas

The family of common fleas is ideally adapted to its habitats, which are the bodies of mammals and birds. The mouthparts are modified to pierce skin and suck blood. Fleas have narrow bodies, perfect for moving about between hairs. Their legs are long and strong, and they have a special spring built into their bodies which acts as an energy store, so they are great jumpers. *Ctenocephalides felis* (Cat Flea (shown here) can high-jump around 200 times its own body length – about 34 cm. If a human could equal that, they would make a jump of 350 metres! Females lay their eggs on the ground and the larvae emerge. When they change to pupae, they can remain like that for years until a suitable animal comes along.

Order: Siphonaptera
Family: Pulicidae
UK species: 9 – World species: 200
Body length: 1–6 mm

Flesh Flies

These flies live in a variety of habitats where they are able to feed on flower nectar, aphids' honeydew or sap flowing from tree wounds. The adult females give birth to larvae and do not lay eggs. The food of species in the family varies: many feed on carrion (dead and rotting flesh). Some are parasites on beetles, grasshoppers and caterpillars of moths and butterflies, and some parasitize turtles and frogs. They look a little like blow flies (see page 19), but are striped dull grey and black; they are never metallic. Some species are used to control insect pests.

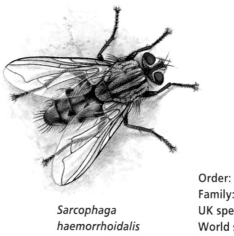

Sarcophaga haemorrhoidalis

Order: Diptera
Family: Sarcophagidae
UK species: 55
World species: 2,100
Body length: 2–20 mm

Bot & Warble Flies

The flies in this family are very heavy-bodied and look a little like honey or bumble bees. They often have hairy abdomens. *Oestris ovis* (Sheep Bot Fly, shown here) gives you a good idea of the bot fly's appearance. Their habitat tends to be close to their host species. In some species the males gather on hilltops for mating purposes.

Warble flies fasten their eggs very firmly to hairs on the legs of cattle, and the larvae burrow under the skin into the animal's back. When mature, they chew their way out and pupate in the soil, leaving a terrible sore.

Order: Diptera
Family: Oestridae
UK species: 10
World species: 160
Body length: 8–25 mm

Louse Flies

These strange-looking flies live as parasites, sucking blood from the bodies of birds or mammals, including deer, cattle, sheep and horses. They have long, curved claws, which hold on to the fur or feathers of their active and moving habitat, and short antennae. As wings and eyes are not needed for their way of life, many species of the family have lost them. The female lays fully grown larvae which have grown inside her body feeding of special 'milk glands'. The mature larvae of *Melophagus ovinus* (Sheep Ked, shown here) attach themselves to the sheep's wool by using a special glue before pupating.

Order: Diptera
Family: Hippoboscidae
UK species: 10
World species: 200
Body length: 1.5–12 mm, mostly 4–7 mm

Parasites

Stylopids

These small parasites are seldom seen because of their way of life. The males look a bit like beetles. The females are grub-like and live on their hosts, especially mining bees, sand wasps and the social wasps (see pages 22–23). Their larvae crawl into flowers, where they wait to hitch a ride on a suitable host. Once aboard, they bore into the body and feed on its internal organs without killing it. After pupation in the host's body, the males fly away, but the females remain, with the tip of the body sticking out as shown here. The odour they give off attracts males to mate with them.

Order: Strepsiptera
Family: Stylopidae
UK species: 13
World species: 260
Body length: 0.5–4 mm

Stylops melittae

Bee Flies

You should look out for these hairy, bee-like flies on a sunny day. They can often be seen flying, hovering and sucking nectar from primroses and celandines. Do not worry about their bee-like buzzing –they have no sting. They lay eggs in the burrows of solitary bees and wasps; their larvae are parasitic on them, as well as beetles, moths and other flies. The pupae have sharp teeth at one end, which break open the seal of the host cell so that the adult fly may escape.

Order: Diptera
Family: Bombyliidae
UK species: 12
World species: 5,000
Body length: 2–28 mm

Bombylius major

Parasitic Flies

The majority of these look like bristly house flies but some are very much larger, very hairy and look rather like bees. They can be found in a variety of habitats drinking nectar, tree sap or honeydew (the *Voria ruralis* secretion from aphids), but they are very active and hard to catch. All their larvae are parasitic upon other insects; the adults lay their eggs on or inside the host's body. The hosts may be butterflies, beetles, grasshoppers, bugs, bees, wasps or flies. Parasitic flies are such efficient controllers of certain insect pests that many are used – and others are under investigation – as biological control agents.

Order: Diptera – Family: Tachinidae
UK species: 235 – World species: 7,800
Body length: 5–15 mm

Fairyflies

This family of tiny wasps contains some of the smallest insects on earth. The females lay their eggs inside the eggs of dragonflies, grasshoppers, butterflies and moths, beetles and flies. One species, *Caraphractus cinctus* (shown here), uses its wings to swim through the water to reach the submerged eggs of giant water beetles. They can remain under water for days at a time. These wasps are a wonderful example of the unseen world of insects and a real challenge for every 'bug hunter'.

Order: Hymenoptera
Family: Mymaridae
UK species: 87
World species: 1,300
Body length: 0.2–2 mm

Braconid Wasps

Brown, reddish-brown or black, these wasps have quite slender bodies. They parasitize other insects; *Apanteles glomeratus* (shown here) searches out the larvae of the Cabbage White Butterfly to lay its eggs in them. The larvae then feed on the body of the host. Finally, some thirty or more larvae emerge and spin yellowish silken cocoons on the outside of the host's body in late summer or early autumn. Search for these 'mummified' caterpillars on cabbage leaves and other foliage, or on the walls of sheds and buildings. Leaving Cabbage White caterpillars in small tubes over the winter may also provide you with some parasitic flies (see opposite). Many species from this family are used as biological control agents.

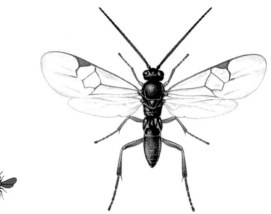

Order: Hymenoptera
Family: Braconidae
UK species: 1,050
World species: 15,000
Body length: 2–15 mm, mostly under 7 mm

Encyrtid Wasps

The majority of these wasps are to be found close to their hosts, which can be scale insects, mealy bugs, aphids and whiteflies. They lay their eggs in the bodies of both immature and adult stages. Despite being so tiny, some of them lay eggs that divide repeatedly at a very early stage in their growth to produce between 10 and 2,000 larvae from a single egg. Others parasitize the larvae of braconid wasps (see above) which are already living as parasites in another larva. *Habrolepis dalmani* (shown here) has been used to control a scale insect (see page 76) that damages oak trees.

Order: Hymenoptera – Family: Encyrtidae
UK species: 201 – World species: 3,000
Body length: 0.5–4 mm, mostly 1–2 mm

Ruby-tailed, Cuckoo or Jewel Wasps

This family is well named because they are so beautiful. The body can be bright blue, green, red, copper or mixed patterns, all with a shining metallic hue. On a hot, sunny day look along fences, sheltered walls or banks where solitary bees and wasps may be living. They are parasites, searching for larval burrows in which to lay their eggs, giving rise to their other name: cuckoo wasps. However, they do not always eat their host, which is first paralysed, but eat its food supply instead. Some species parasitize sawfly larva (see page 17), and a few eat praying mantis eggs (see page 30).

Chrysis fuscipennis
These wasps often roll themselves into a ball as a protection against predators.

Order: Hymenoptera – Family: Chrysididae
UK Species: 33 – World species: 3,000
Body length: 3–18 mm

Parasites

Eulophid Wasps

These very tiny wasps are able to find many kinds of hidden larvae, like the leaf blotch-miner moths' larvae (see page 46). They kill these larvae by laying eggs in their bodies. They are an important link in the chain of life because they help to control natural insect populations such as those of moths, beetles, aphids and scale insects. Today some species are bred and released into the environment to help control insect pests of larch and pine trees.

Baryscapus bruchophagi

Order: Hymenoptera – Family: Eulophidae
UK species: 391 – World species: 3,100
Body length: 0.5-5mm, mostly 1–3 mm

Pteromalid Wasps

All known pteromalid wasps are either black or a very metallic blue or green. Being parasitic, they are found everywhere that their host species live. A few form galls, while some are herbivores or hunt small insects, such as the larvae of the gall midge or the eggs of other insect species. The larvae of one world species destroys house flies and related insects, while another attacks fleas. These wasps are good examples of the useful work carried on by a tiny insect which very few of us have ever seen. There are still many undescribed species.

Order: Hymenoptera
Family: Pteromalidae
UK species: 532
World species: 3,200
Body length: 1–8 mm

Pteromalus dolichurus

Ichneumon Wasps

If you see a long, narrow-bodied insect waving its antennae as it crawls about on a flat-topped flower, you may have found an ichneumon wasp. Most of the females have an ovipositor (long egg-laying tube). The picture shows *Rhyssa persuasoria* using her antennae to scent out and find the larva of a wood wasp (see page 44), which tunnels along tree trunks. When she finds one, she uses her ovipositor as a drill to bore down to the larva and place an egg on its body. It hatches, and then her larva feeds on the body of the wood wasp larva. By sweeping your net among wild flowers, especially in damp habitats, you may find some of these wasps.

Rhyssa persuasoria ovipositing –
the slender ovipositor can either
follow the host's tunnels or drill
directly through the timber.

Order: Hymenoptera – Family: Ichenumonidae
UK species: 2,000 – World species: 20,000
Body length: 3–42 mm

Platygastrid Wasps

Most species of platygastrid wasps lay eggs in the eggs or very young larvae of gall midges (see page 77), mealy bugs (see page 75) or whiteflies (see page 75). Species of *Inostemma* (shown here) have a forward pointing 'handle' which contains the ovipositor. Their habitats are widespread, but are closely interlinked with the presence of whatever may be their host species. The life history of many species of these very small, shiny, black insects is still unknown.

Order: Hymenoptera – Family: Platygastridae
UK species: 150 – World species: 950
Body length:
0.5–4 mm

Scelonid Wasps

Like the platygastrid wasps, scelonid wasps have bent or elbowed antennae. Most of the adults are solitary and lay their eggs in the newly laid eggs of moths and butterflies. To be sure of such freshness these wasps have evolved the habit of clinging to the host insect until she lays her eggs. Some even lose their wings once they have found and boarded a suitable host insect. The species shown here, *Telenomus dalmanni*, parasitizes moth eggs.

Order: Hymenoptera
Family: Scelonidae
UK species: 102
World species: 1,250
Body length: 1–14 mm, mostly under 4 mm

Torymid Wasps

As these wasps are very small; the best way to find them is to rear some galls (see page 73). To sort them from other wasps that may also emerge, look for wasps with bright, shiny, metallic blue or green bodies. They will also have bent antennae and the ovipositor may be as long as, or even longer than, the rest of the body. While some species form galls, others parasitize caterpillars, solitary bee's and wasp's larvae, and some lay their eggs in the seeds of conifers, hawthorn, apple and pear.

Torymus varians

Order: Hymenoptera – Family: Torymidae
UK species: 75 – World species: 1,500
Body length: 1–8 mm

Trichogrammatid Wasps

These lay their eggs into the eggs of a variety of other insects. To observe these tiny wasps you will need to collect insect eggs and wait to see what emerges. It is possible that one of them will be an undescribed species. The habits of many are still unknown. The females of some species swim under water in search of the eggs of dragonflies and aquatic insects. Some species are very useful in controlling pest species.

Order: Hymenoptera
Family: Trichogrammatidae
UK species: 29
World species: 532
Body length:
0.3–1.2 mm

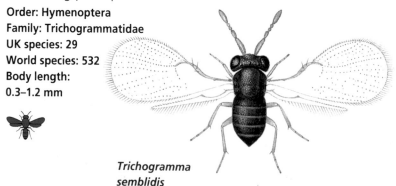

Trichogramma semblidis

Keeping Insects at Home

Have you ever thought of having your own insect zoo at home? Many kinds are easy to keep and it is great fun watching their behaviour in close up. However, you should only collect insects to observe them. Don't keep them more than 2–3 days, and always release them back into the habitat that you caught them in.

The rules for success are:
1 **Always handle insects very gently** – their legs and wings are often delicate.
2 **Keep the cage away from direct sunlight** and away from radiators.
3 **Provide small air holes in the lid** or use fine netting. Insects breathe just as other animals do.
4 **Provide fresh food daily** and remove all uneaten food at the same time.
5 **Clean out the cages regularly**.

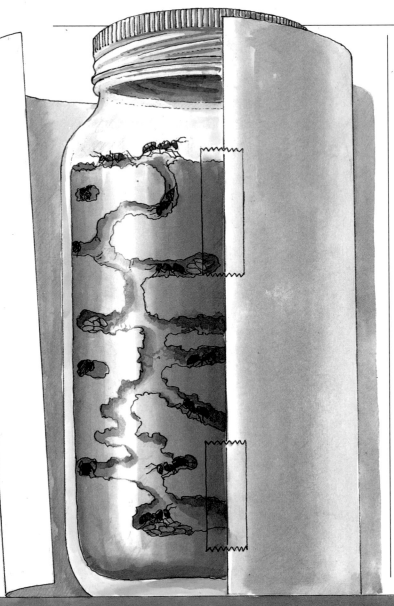

Insect cages

The best cages for insect watching are large jam jars or preserving jars. If you are using the metal screw-on top as its lid, ask an adult to punch 6 to 8 small air holes into it. Or you can use a piece of fine material, like nylon, Terylene or muslin, with a strong elastic band. Always put some leaves in the bottom of the jar, and a twig, so that the insects have some shelter. For a larger cage, like a fish tank, bend a wire coat hanger into an approximate rectangle and fix the material on to it with staples. You must weight the corners to prevent escapes.

Ant nest

You can easily make an ant home from a large glass jar. Partly fill it with soil and cover the outside with lightproof paper. Make sure the lid is antproof.
1 **Dig up a garden ant nest** and try to find the biggest ant (a queen). Wear gloves as the worker ants will try to defend her.
2 **Put the queen in her new home** with as many workers as you can collect.
3 **Feed them every day** with a little sugar or honey sprinkled on the soil surface.
4 **In time they will excavate tunnels against the glass.** Remove the paper around the jar from time to time to see how they are doing.

What's inside?

Many different insects make galls. Why not collect and hatch them? In spring Gall Wasps (see page 45) lay their eggs on the buds of oak trees, which causes brown marble-like galls to form. Inside the galls, the wasp larvae are growing, and in the autumn, the adult wasps will eat their way out and fly off.

1 **Look for galls** on the ground in woods, on oaks, and many other plants and trees. Collect them in late summer and autumn.
2 **Cut the twig or plant stem** so that it fits into a jam jar.
3 **Cover the mouth of each jar** with a square of fabric and secure it with an elastic band.
4 **Put the jars in your garage**, tool shed or on a balcony for the winter.
5 **In the spring, watch** for the tiny adult insects to emerge.

Mini vivarium

You can make a wonderful ever-changing habitat in an old fish tank or large plastic sweet jar. By using stones, fallen leaves, a clump of grass, soil or sand you can make a home for grasshoppers and beetles. Long-horned Grasshoppers (see page 40) will live well in a grassy tank with some branches for it to crawl about on. If you have two of these crickets, you will most likely hear them singing after dark. Always release them after a few days.

Earwig nest

Earwigs (see page 15) will live quite comfortably in a plastic sandwich box. Put moist – not wet – soil on the bottom with a couple of flat stones or a piece of bark for them to hide under. Add some ground litter in one corner. If you keep some between January and March they may lay their eggs. They will need tiny pieces of raw meat and bits of lettuce, cucumber or a slice of apple as food.

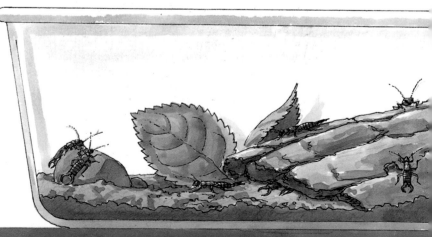

House & Plant Pests

Silverfish & Firebrats

You may see some of these small, wingless, greyish or silver-scaled insects running about the kitchen or bathroom at night. The rear end has three tail-like filaments and they feed on flour, damp textiles, book bindings and wallpaper paste. Household spiders enjoy eating them. Most species live outdoors, so look for them under stones, in debris and in ants' nests. They run for cover very fast, which often saves their lives. *Lepisma saccharina* (Silverfish, shown here) prefers cool, damp habitats, while firebrats often stay near hot pipes and ovens.

Order: Thysanura – Family: Lepismatidae
UK species: 2
World species: 200
Body length:
8–20 mm

German Cockroaches

Members of this family look shiny and are generally brown or light brown in colour. They have long, slender legs and long, thin antennae. Although they have wings, they seldom fly. A female lays an average of five egg cases and each one may contain about forty eggs. From each of these a young cockroach emerges which looks exactly like a small adult. *Blattella germanica* (German Cockroach, shown here) counts as a major household pest. They have an unpleasant smell, which will be obvious to you if they are around.

Order: Blattodea
Family: Blattellidae
UK species: 4
World species: 1,750
Body length: 8–25 mm,
mostly about 15 mm

Clothes Moths

You may find some species from this family around rotting wood and fungi in a variety of habitats, but they are most common indoors where their larvae feed on woollen fabrics, fur and textiles. The female *Tineola bisselliella* (Webbing Clothes Moth, shown here) lays about 100 eggs in the folds of clothing. When the larvae emerge, they spin a tube made from the gnawed material as a protection against drying out. With the increase of man-made fibres and repellents, many are becoming scarcer, though some remain serious pests, particularly in museums.

Order: Lepidoptera
Family: Tineidae
UK species: 47
World species: 2,500
Body length: 8–20 mm

Bed Bugs

These blood-sucking bugs have oval, flattened bodies, and some have a covering of silky hairs. They are parasitic on humans, other mammals and birds. Where humans live in crowded and insanitary places, they are common. At night they suck the blood of their hosts and return to their hiding places. In a single meal an adult *Cimes lectularius* (Bed Bug, shown here) can suck up seven times its own weight of blood. The nymphs take from 6–26 weeks to develop – they need a blood meal at each of the five moults during their growth.

Order: Hemiptera
Family: Cimicidae
UK species: 4
World species: 90
Body length: 3–6 mm

Soft, Wax & Tortoise Scales

In general, scale insects are oval and flattened and have a hard waxy or smooth body. Most of the females remain fixed in one place on a plant and do not look like an insect at all. *Coccus hesperidum* (Brown Soft Scale, shown here) is a pest of citrus trees and greenhouse crops. A single female may produce hundreds of millions of eggs in one year. From these emerge nymphs, called 'crawlers', who move away from their mother before pushing their 'beaks' into the plant to suck sap. Many nymphs produce wax filaments that allow them to lift off on the wind and travel great distances.

Order: Hemiptera – Family: Coccidae
UK Species: 35 – World species: 1,250
Body length: 2–12 mm

Whiteflies

If your parents have a greenhouse, or simply keep a few house plants at home, you may have heard about the whitefly problem. The females of *Trialeurodes vaporariorum* (Greenhouse Whitefly, shown here) lay eggs on the underside of leaves. The nymphs suck the plant sap and excrete honeydew. In turn this sugary fluid attracts a fungus (*Botrytis*) which covers the plant in black smudges. A whitefly population explosion can be controlled by using a small parasitic wasp called *Encarsia formosa*. This is cheaper and safer than using chemicals.

Order: Hemiptera
Family: Aleyrodidae
UK species: 19
World species: 1,200
Body length: 1–3 mm

Mealy Bugs

Unlike other scale insects, members of this family have legs at all stages in their lifecycle. The females are wingless and are covered in a mealy or waxy white coating. The males look more like proper insects with a pair of wings, but their mouthparts are undeveloped so they cannot feed. All mealy bug species are sap suckers. The females of some species lay eggs, but others give birth to live nymphs. Mealy bugs are found on a variety of host plants; each species tends to keep to a particular type of plant.

Order: Hemiptera
Family: Pseudococcidae
UK Species: 35
World species: 2,000
Body length: 5–8 mm

Pseudococcus adonidum

Squash or Leaf-footed Bugs

The males of some species have strong hind legs armed with spines. These are used in territorial fighting for access to females. All species are herbivorous (plant-eating) and defend themselves by spraying a pungent, unpleasant fluid at their enemies. Some species are pests on squash and gourd plants, which gives them their name, and other crops, but others may be found feeding on St John's wort, grasses and other plants.

Order: Hemiptera
Family: Coreidae
UK species: 10
World species: 2,000
Body length: 10–40 mm

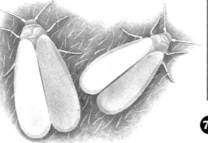

Coriomeris scabricornis

House & Plant Pests

Skin, Larder & Museum Beetles

This family of small beetles can be found in a huge variety of indoor and outdoor habitats. Their food, when larvae, is mainly the dried remains of plants or animals, including hair and feathers. Others thrive on a diet of carpets, fur, spices or dried milk. Many museum collections of organic (plant- or animal-based) materials have been destroyed by *Anthrenus verbasci* (Museum Beetle, shown here). The adults mostly eat pollen from flowers.

Order: Coleoptera – Family: Dermestidae
UK species: 16 – World species: 800
Body length: 1–12 mm

Scarab Beetles & their relatives

The Sacred Scarabs of ancient Egypt are part of this family. Their habitat is extremely varied, but includes fungi, flowers, dung, under bark and in nests of ants, termites and vertebrates. There are many sub-families with common names like dung beetles, cockchafers, skin beetles, rose chafers, rhinoceros and hercules beetles. In early summer you may see and hear a common cockchafer flying towards a lighted window on a warm night. Rose Chafers are a beautiful shining green with a golden gloss and can be seen on summer flowers.

Serica brunnea

Order: Coleoptera
Family: Scarabaeidae
UK species: 89
World species: 20,000
Body length: 2–150 mm

Pea & Bean Weevils

These pests of stored products lay their eggs on seeds and these produce whitish grub-like larvae that burrow into peas and beans. Many larvae may develop inside a single seed, thus destroying it. When fully grown, they pupate near the surface and on emergence they chew their way out. This action leaves a small round hole – a sure sign that the culprit was a pea or bean weevil. Some species attack crops in the field, like *Callosobruchus maculatus* (Cowpea Weevil, shown here).

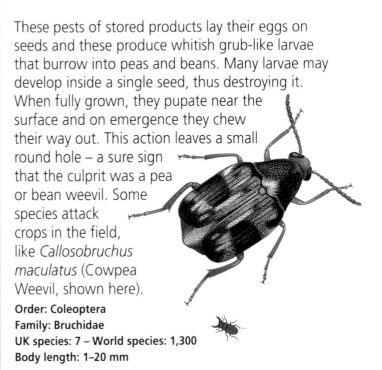

Order: Coleoptera
Family: Bruchidae
UK species: 7 – World species: 1,300
Body length: 1–20 mm

Click Beetles or Skip Jacks

These beetles have the ability to click loudly and throw themselves into the air when lying on their backs. The very loud click and the sudden movement will frighten any predator, while moving the beetle out of harm's way. You may find one in your beating tray, especially from oak trees. They are also found on the ground under leaf litter and in decaying wood. The larvae are called wireworms, because they are thin and tough-bodied. They are found under bark, in rotten wood and in soil.

Order: Coleoptera
Family: Elateridae
UK species: 65
World species: 8,500
Body length: 2–60 mm

Agriotes lineatus

Gall Midges

Many members of this family lay eggs in the leaves of plants and so make galls form in the daisy, grass and willow families. They can be found anywhere that their host plants grow. Some species of gall midges produce larvae that are parasitic on small insect mites, while others are predators. A few species live in fungi, and some even live in galls made by other insects.

Mayetiola destructor (Hessian Fly) – the larvae is a pest on wheat, rye and barley, particularly in southern Europe.

Order: Diptera – Family: Cecidomyiidae
UK species: 620 – World species: 4,600
Body length: 1–8 mm

Lesser Fruit or Pomace Flies

Tiny flies of this family have been studied in more detail than any other animal. They are of immense help in the study of genetics because they are small, can be easily bred on artificial foods, and reproduce very fast. In the wild they are found near rotting fruit and in food and drink processing factories. Search around decaying, fallen apples for tiny flies with red eyes that look like the one shown here (*Drosophilia funebris*), to find them.

Order: Diptera
Family: Drosophilidae
UK species: 52
World species: 2,900
Body length: 1–6 mm

Clearwings or Clear-winged Moths

These moths are truly amazing. They mimic social wasps, bees or ichneumon wasps, and resemble them very closely in body shape and colour. Even their wings are almost free of scales to increase the illusion. *Sesia apiformis* (Hornet Clearwing Moth, shown here) mimics a hornet. They complete the mimicry by buzzing, and some species even pretend to sting, so if you see one, look carefully and make sure it is a clearwing and not a wasp. They can be seen around flowers in a variety of habitats.

Order: Lepidoptera
Family: Sesiidae
UK species: 15 – World species: 1,000
Wingspan: 14–40 mm

Gelechiid Moths

These small to tiny moths form one of the largest moth families. The caterpillars of some species protect themselves by rolling leaves into a tube fastened with their silk. Others spin shelters of silk in the leaves, shoots or flower heads of host plants. By searching carefully and looking closely at a number of oak leaves in late summer you should be able to find some of these leaf-rollers. Many species are pests on crops, such as potatoes, tomatoes, strawberries and soft fruit.

Order: Lepidoptera
Family: Gelechiidae
UK species: 145
World species: 4,200
Wingspan: 7–27 mm

Metzneria lappella

Find Out Some More

Useful organizations

The best organization for you to get in touch with is your local County Wildlife Trust. There are forty-seven of these trusts in Great Britain and you should contact them if you want to know about nature reserves and activities in your area. Ask your local library for their address, or contact:

The Wildlife Trusts, The Green, Witham Park, Waterside South, Lincoln LN5 7JR (0522–544400).

WATCH is the junior branch of The Wildlife Trusts. Local WATCH groups run meetings all over the country. Again you can find out about your nearest WATCH group by contacting the The Wildlife Trusts.

Your local **natural history society** may organize walks to find and study insects. They are led by local experts and you will find them of great help. Your local library will have a list of them.

The Bug Club, c/o Dr C Betts, Hatherly Laboratories, Prince of Wales Road, Exeter, Devon EX4 4PS. They issue a Bug Club Newsletter, *The Bug News*, full of ideas for things to do. Their membership pack includes details of reduced admission prices to wildlife attractions in the UK.

Amateur Entomologist's Society, 8 Heather Close, New Haw, Weybridge, Surrey KT15 3PF

The Cambridge Ladybird Survey, c/o Dr M.E.N. Majerus, Department of Genetics Field Station, 219d Huntingdon Road, Cambridge CB3 ODL. They issue a periodic magazine with notes and articles on ladybirds. There are plenty of ideas on how you can help.

The Nature Conservancy Council, Calthorpe House, Calthorpe Street, Banbury, Oxon, OX16 8EX will send you a list of local Nature Reserves. Many of these reserves have Interpretive Centres to explain the wildlife present there. They may also have information on rare insects to be found on the reserve.

The British Trust for Conservation Volunteers (BTCV), 36 St Mary's Street, Wallingford, Oxon OX10 0EU (0491–39766). They work in partnership with landowner, local communities, councils, businesses and charities to protect and maintain rare habitats, footpaths and nature trails. They publish a quarterly magazine, called *The Conserver,* which keeps members up to date with the latest news. They also have a School Membership Scheme; ask your teacher to find out about this.

Useful books

Collin's Guide to Wildlife in House and Home by H. Mourier & O. Winding (Collins, 1986).

Collin's Guide to Insects of Britain and Western Europe by M. Chinery (Collins, 1986).

Creepy Crawlies by C. Kilpatrick (Usborne First Nature Guides, 1990).

Field Guide to Caterpillars of Butterflies and Moths in Britain and Europe by D. Carter & B. Hargreaves (Collins,).

Fields and Hedgerows by M. Chinery (EXPLORING THE COUNTRYSIDE series, Kingfisher, 1982).

Insects of the Northern Hemisphere by G. McGavin and R. Lewington (Dragon's World, 1992).

NATURALISTS' HANDBOOK SERIES – 8 separate titles about insects (Richmond Publishing Co. Ltd).

Pocket Guide to Butterflies of Britain & Europe by J Feltwell & B Hargreaves (Dragon's World, 1994).

Pocket Guide to Insects of the Northern Hemisphere by G. McGavin and R. Lewington (Dragon's World, 1992). Handy spiral-bound guide.

A Step-by-Step Book about Stick Insects by D. Alderton (TFH Publications, 1992).

WATCH Really Useful Insect Pack (Richmond Publishing Co. Ltd).

WATCH Really Useful Damsels and Dragons Pack (Richmond Publishing Co. Ltd).

Index

Places to visit:

Insects are all around you, wherever you go. If you would like to learn more about them and observe them, try visiting the following places: Butterfly farms, nature reserves, local parks and nature trails. Ask if your local zoo has an insect house.
Many museums have insect collections. Try:

British Museum of Natural History, Cromwell Road, London SW7 5BD. (071–938 9123).

City of Bristol Museum and Art Gallery, Queen's Road, Bristol BS8 1RL (0272–299771).

National Museum of Wales, Cathays Park, Cardiff, CF1 3NP (0222–397951).

Oxford University Museum, Parks Road, Oxford OX1 3PW (0865–272950).

Royal Museum of Scotland, Chambers Street, Edinburgh EH1 1JF (031–225 7534).

The Zoological Museum, Akerman Street, Tring, Herts HP23 6AB (044–282 4181).

Index

Glossary

abdomen the third section of an insect's body. It carries the *ovipositor* and the sting (see opposite the title page)

carnivorous any animal that eats meat 58

enzymes natural substances produced by the body to speed up chemical reactions in the body (for example to help you digest your food) 12

herbivorous any animal that eats plants 10

larva or larvae a young stage of the more complex insects when it looks very different to the adult (like a caterpillar which later becomes a butterfly) 12

nymph the young stage of a large group of winged insects. They look very much like the adult insect 54

omnivorous any animal which eats both plants and other animals 58

ovipositor the egg-laying device on the *abdomen* of the adult female insect. In some insects it also acts as a sting 70

rostrum the tubular, slender, sucking mouthpieces of some insects 13

secretion a substance produced by a gland in the body, often containing *enzymes* 10

thorax the middle section of an insect's body. It is divided into three segments, each of which carries a pair of legs. The back two carry the wings if they exist (see opposite the title page)

viviparous giving birth to live young, instead of laying eggs 10